# BETWEEN EARTH AND HEAVEN: THE ARCHITECTURE OF JOHN LAUTNER

HAMMER · RIZZOLI NEW YORK

BETWEEN EARTH AND HEAVEN:

# THE ARCHITECTURE OF JOHN LAUTNER

EDITED BY Nicholas Olsberg TEXTS BY Jean-Louis Cohen, Nicholas Olsberg, and Frank Escher

RIZZOLI INTERNATIONAL PUBLICATIONS IN ASSOCIATION WITH HAMMER MUSEUM

First published in the United States of America in 2008 by
RIZZOLI INTERNATIONAL PUBLICATIONS, INC.
300 Park Avenue South
New York, New York 10010
www.rizzoliusa.com

In association with
HAMMER MUSEUM
10899 Wilshire Boulevard
Los Angeles, California 90024
www.hammer.ucla.edu

This publication accompanies the exhibition *Between Earth and Heaven: The Architecture of John Lautner*, organized by Frank Escher and Nicholas Olsberg and presented at the Hammer Museum, Los Angeles, July 13–October 12, 2008.

The exhibition *Between Earth and Heaven: The Architecture of John Lautner* is made possible through a major gift from the Dunard Fund USA. Generous support has also been provided by the Lloyd E. Rigler—Lawrence E. Deutsch Foundation and Helen and Sam Zell.

It has also been made possible, in part, by the 1011 Foundation, Inc., Bobby Kotick; the Harriett and Richard Gold/Gold Family Foundation; Ronnie and Vidal Sassoon; and by a grant from the Graham Foundation for Advanced Studies in the Fine Arts.

Additional support has been provided by Michael W. LaFetra; Trina Turk and Jonathan Skow; Adele Yellin; and the City of Los Angeles, Department of Cultural Affairs.

The catalogue is published with the assistance of The Brotman Foundation of California and The Getty Foundation.

The Hammer Museum is operated and partially funded by the University of California, Los Angeles. Occidental Petroleum Corporation has partially endowed the Museum and constructed the Occidental Petroleum Cultural Center Building, which houses the Museum.

ISBN: 978-0-8478-3014-5
Library of Congress Control Number: 2007926994

Designed by Volume Inc.

Front endpapers: Mar Brisas, Acapulco, Mexico, 1973, courtesy of the John Lautner Archive, Research Library, The Getty Research Institute, Los Angeles (2007.M.13).
© The John Lautner Foundation
Page 1: Mar Brisas, Acapulco, Mexico, 1973, courtesy of the John Lautner Archive, Research Library, The Getty Research Institute, Los Angeles (2007.M.13). © The John Lautner Foundation.
Pages 2-3: Silvertop, Los Angeles, 1963 (detail), courtesy of the John Lautner Archive, Research Library, The Getty Research Institute, Los Angeles (2007.M.13). © The John Lautner Foundation.
Pages 4-5: Malibu Cliff House, Malibu, California, 1990, courtesy of the John Lautner Archive, Research Library, The Getty Research Institute, Los Angeles (2007.M.13).
© The John Lautner Foundation
Back endpapers: Hope House, Palm Springs, California, 1979, courtesy of the John Lautner Archive, Research Library, The Getty Research Institute, Los Angeles (2007.M.13).
© The John Lautner Foundation

Distributed to the U.S. trade by Random House, New York
Printed and bound in China

2008 2009 2010 2011 2012 / 10 9 8 7 6 5 4 3 2 1

ERRATA
Due to an editorial error, the Lautner house in Acapulco has been incorrectly identified throughout this edition as Mar Brisas. The correct name for the house is Marbrisa. We apologize for the error.

# CONTENTS

# FOREWORD

John Lautner, as described by Frederic Lyman, was an artist in a distinctly Whitmanesque American tradition—"a sardonic, self-confident, stubborn, shaggy individualist."[1] Along with many other such lone wolves, Lautner claimed to dislike Los Angeles intensely, yet found in this city what he needed most—a culture ready to run artistic risks. Ironically, the three things Lautner liked least about Southern California—its "fast food, fast deals, fast everything"; its culture of superficial sensationalizing; and its vulgar displays of luxury—are the three with which he is, mistakenly, most identified. He has been both scorned and admired for his infamous coffee-shop "Googie" style at the start of his career, which he did little to originate and much to correct. The logical, humane, and poetic experiments in structuring space in his middle years have been misunderstood either as wondrous Space Age fantasies or as dystopic visions of a *Blade Runner* future. And his later houses, with their meditative and transcendent play between vista and shelter, have been dismissed—largely with nothing but their budgets in mind—as typical showplaces of Hollywood extravaganza. This exhibition and publication aims to set the record straight.

John Lautner's fascination with new shapes and structures had nothing to do with Space Age futurism, or movieland glamour, or virtuoso engineering, but came from his determination to humanize the spaces of the built world and create an endlessly varied organic poetry. This was a profoundly serious agenda. It was grounded in his belief that carefully considered spaces can awaken a transcendental sense of the environment. Scrupulously democratic, he was as concerned with the modest family home and the bachelor suite as with the luxury retreat, making a massive contribution to new ideas for the postwar suburban dwelling. He brought to architecture an innovative and expressive emotional force through his adventuresome use of structure, form, and materials.

The essays that follow draw for the first time on Lautner's writings, letters, and papers to show the deep resonance of his work with other progressive architectural thinking in his time; his strong grounding in a world of ideas; the extent to which he shared the same individualistic mental, aesthetic, and moral landscapes as other pioneering American artists of his day; and the prescience of his new structural, spatial, and formal ideas. Tracing the evolution of his work through the first comprehensive study and presentation of his drawings, sketches, studies, notes, and models, the essays go on to demonstrate the originality of his ideas regarding sites, shaping spaces, and experiments with structure.

[1] Frederic Lyman, nominating Lautner to be a Fellow of the American Institute of Architects (AIA), John Lautner Foundation Archives, 1971.

By looking in this new, more expansive and inquiring fashion at an iconic but often misrepresented figure in the architectural history of Los Angeles, the authors of this volume have done what the Hammer Museum sets out to do in all its programs: to deepen knowledge of the city's art and design history; to encourage recognition both of the originality of the region's culture and of the vital part it has long played in the exchange of new art and design ideas worldwide; and to incite an understanding that art and design operate within the broadest intellectual and social context and are a central expression—whether sardonic or idealistic (and Lautner was both)—of the civilization that produces them.

The curators of this exhibition, Frank Escher and Nicholas Olsberg, have both generously shared their insights into Lautner and his profound importance, and for this and their endless enthusiasm and perseverance I am so grateful. I would also like to thank the John Lautner Foundation, especially Karol Lautner Peterson, Judith Lautner, Christopher Carr, and Duncan Nicholson, for all of their assistance in realizing this project. And I am especially appreciative of Jenée Misraje, Lilian Pfaff, Ali Subotnick, and the entire staff at the Hammer who have made this project more than a far-off dream.

I would also like to express my appreciation to the funders of this exhibition for their belief in the importance of this undertaking. I am extremely grateful to the Dunard Fund USA, the Lloyd E. Rigler—Lawrence E. Deutsch Foundation, and Helen and Sam Zell, who were immediately supportive of this project. Harriett and Richard Gold/Gold Family Foundation and Ronnie and Vidal Sassoon have been longtime friends of the Hammer and each made significant gifts to this exhibition. I am also appreciative of the generosity of Bobby Kotick and the 1011 Foundation, Inc. I would additionally like to recognize the leadership of the Graham Foundation for Advanced Studies in the Fine Arts for supporting this and other architecture exhibitions in the United States. My additional thanks go to Michael W. LaFetra, Trina Turk and Jonathan Skow, Adele Yellin, and the City of Los Angeles, Department of Cultural Affairs. Lastly, I am grateful to The Getty Foundation for their ongoing support of Hammer publications, and to Toni Brotman Wald and Lowell Marks and The Brotman Foundation of California for an early gift that was critical to the production of this publication, which will stand as a testament to the remarkable beauty and lasting impact of John Lautner's architecture.

This long overdue exhibition recognizes one of North America's greatest visionaries, and we hope it will inspire generations of art lovers, architects, and designers to come.

ANN PHILBIN, DIRECTOR

# ACKNOWLEDGMENTS

The curators of *Between Earth and Heaven: The Architecture of John Lautner* would like to extend their deepest thanks to all those who participated in its preparation.

We would first like to thank the director of the Hammer Museum, Ann Philbin, for her singular vision and confidence in John Lautner's work, which propelled the long and fruitful process that led to the project's realization at the Hammer.

The John Lautner Foundation and the members of its board, including Karol Lautner Peterson and Judith Lautner, deserve particular mention for their generosity of time, effort, and input throughout the project.

John Lautner's architectural archive (consisting of drawings, models, photographs, and project files) was donated in 2007 by the John Lautner Foundation to the Getty Research Institute in Los Angeles. There the archive joins other archives of Southern California architects, such as Pierre Koenig and Ray Kappe, and that of the architectural photographer Julius Shulman. The Getty Research Institute and its staff, in particular Wim de Wit, Albrecht Gumlich, Irene Lotspeich-Phillips, and Mary Reinsch Sackett, have been supportive and wonderful to work with, and it is heartening to know that the archive has found such a deserving home.

The exhibition could not have been possible without its generous lenders. To Karol Lautner Peterson, Dr. and Mrs. Carl Pearlman, and, of course, the John Lautner Foundation and Archive, we extend our deepest appreciation. The current and previous homeowners of John Lautner's houses have been extremely giving of their time, particularly Mike Kilroy, Agnes and Nancy Pearlman, Milton Sidley, Benedikt and Lauren Taschen, and Douglas and Octavia Walstrom.

Eric Heiman and his staff at Volume, Inc. produced a beautiful design for this publication, and it was a pleasure to work with him. We are also very grateful to Jean-Louis Cohen for the time and energy he devoted to writing the book's brilliant introductory essay. Editors Meera Deean and Dung Ngo of Rizzoli International Publications provided unstinting feedback on the essay texts and the layout of the publication, helping to make it a wonderful accompaniment to the exhibition and an important document in its own right.

At the Hammer Museum, curator Ali Subotnick and exhibition manager Lilian Pfaff provided an incredible amount of support and made certain the project moved forward with an attentive and unfailing diligence. Jenée Misraje, exhibition coordinator, was also an essential force in putting all the pieces together as were curatorial assistant Claire de Dobay Rifelj and interns Sasha Bergstrom-Katz, Bessie Zhu, and Lauren Ino. Peter Gould, chief preparator, and Portland McCormick, senior registrar, with their staff sought to bring our visions to fruition with their careful planning and indispensable precision. Jennifer Wells Green, director of development, and Miranda Carroll, director of communications, and their teams were essential in securing funding and promoting the exhibition. Conservators Lynne Blaikie and Maureen McGee were especially helpful and generous with their expertise and advice.

We also extend our gratitude to the rest of the Hammer Museum staff for supporting the exhibition in countless ways. The curators would also like to thank the following individuals for their ample help along the way: Helena Arahuete, Christopher Carr, Alvin Chen, John Contini, Nora Contini, Blair Ellis, Carol Hogel, Elizabeth Honnold, Bobby Kotick, Leonard Malin, Andrew Nasser, Duncan Nicholson, Ken Reiner, Glen Howard Small, Christine Steiner, Julia Strickland, Vaughan Trammell, John de la Vaux, Elizabeth West, Louis Wiehle, Guy Zebert; Oscar Munoz and Margo Stipe at the Frank Lloyd Wright Foundation Archives; Rosemary Michelin at the Longyear Library, Marquette, Michigan; and John Yoder at Syracuse University. For their assistance with the models and research: Axel Prichard-Schmitzberger, Ruby Carr, Derek Cunha, Gerardo Del Rosal, Lyle Fricke, Miguel Gonzalez, Mike Idoine, Lucas Reames, Lital Shiri, and Josh Venzor at California State Polytechnic University. Special thanks go to filmmaker Murray Grigor, Sara Sackner, Anna Thomas, and Grigor's production crew. And we are particularly grateful to Joshua White and his studio for the stunning new photographs of the archive materials. We are especially appreciative of Ravi GuneWardena for his generous assistance and support.

FRANK ESCHER AND NICHOLAS OLSBERG, CURATORS

Jean-Louis Cohen

# JOHN LAUTNER'S LUXURIANT TECTONICS

*right* John Lautner, Silvertop, Los Angeles, California, 1963
*page 12* John Lautner, Mar Brisas, Acapulco, Mexico, 1973

The four decades during which John Lautner produced his major works were marked by a profound and recurring crisis of confidence in Modern architecture. At first glance, his architecture appears to be quite unconcerned either with the confrontations that marked the critical debates of those times or with the painful self-questioning that troubled its architects, and seems to have developed quite independently of worldwide currents of thinking. In fact, the proud air of isolation that Lautner affected should not in the least suggest an ignorance or distance from what was happening in architecture throughout the Americas, in Europe, and in Japan after World War II. Indeed, the importance and relevance of his work can only be fully grasped in relation to the many different formal ideas then in play. But his work is so firmly inscribed into the specific topographies of Southern California—from its shores to its canyons to its deserts—that it is not always easy to see how its echoes resound from afar.

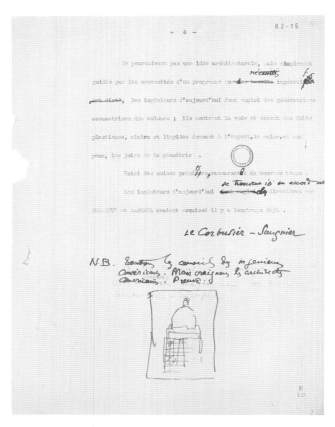

Le Corbusier, page from original manuscript of *Toward an Architecture*, 1923. The handwritten sentence asserts: "Let us heed the advice of American engineers. But let us fear American architects."

Like any significant body of work, Lautner's follows a complicated path. Its turns and junctures derive from the changing practical conditions of his commissions, and they are advanced by developments in his internal thinking; but they also respond to powerful shifts in the dominant discourse of the day. His major built works cannot be divorced from the specific landscapes to which they react and which they do so much to shape. But at the same time, they always turn one facet outward to capture and cast reflections of a much wider discussion, particularly on domestic space and on the structural dimension of architecture.

## A WATCHFUL ISOLATION

By refusing to work within the commercial architectural marketplace of Los Angeles, based on the inevitable but unacceptable principle he called "repeat and repeat," Lautner essentially limited his practice to the service of private clients. The exceptions to this rule—a modest contribution to educational buildings and a very important one to roadside commerce, especially to the budding fast-food industry—are often not very different in scale from his houses.[1]

The individualism of his commissions was reinforced by the isolated individualism of his practice, leading him into constant struggles against the prevailing practices of the Southern California building industry. While both these circumstances encouraged a posture of isolation, Lautner was not in the least indifferent to what was going on in the world of building at large, and he himself would refer to it often. As Frank Escher points out, his attention was most often drawn to structural innovations and thinking—to the work of Pier Luigi Nervi, Eduardo Torroja, Frei Otto, and Félix Candela. It is remarkable to note how much emphasis Lautner indirectly places on the work of engineers, as if recalling the argument of Le Corbusier in *Toward an Architecture* (1923), when he wrote: "Engineers are healthy and virile, active and useful, moral and joyful. Architects are disenchanted and idle, boastful or morose," a myth of the conflict between engineer and architect that was later reinforced in a book of which Lautner could not have been unaware, Sigfried Giedion's *Space, Time, and Architecture*, published in 1941.[2]

Lautner spoke directly of his interest in the projects published in Bruno Zevi's magazine *L'Architettura, cronache e storia*, which started in 1955, and in what he saw in the pages of the *Architectural Review* during its heyday as a critical journal. As for the architecture of Los Angeles, he both rejected the principle of repetition that he saw dominating the widely recognized work of Richard Neutra, and to a certain extent identified with the working methods of Rudolf Schindler, whose contribution—until Esther McCoy revived interest in him in the early 1960s—had largely been forgotten. Indeed, Lautner knew Schindler's work well from the start, joining Frank Lloyd Wright on a tour of the Silver

Lake houses in the late 1930s. Interviewed by Dominique Lyon in 1987, Lautner was very clear on their differences: "Neutra did nothing more than discover one thing, and then repeated it all his life. Schindler's works are more varied, adapted to his clients' needs and to their situations. He was making interesting things, working as his own contractor, and finding ways to build that cut the costs for his clients. I think that is very good."[3]

## AN ANTHOLOGY OF STRUCTURES

Any effort to classify or categorize Lautner's many different ways of shaping architectural form inevitably leads to the identification of parallels that might link them to the investigations of his contemporaries, whether or not those links are apparent in the few words of Lautner's own laconic discourse. His work is part of a new phase in the development of Modern architecture in which the orthogonal solutions that first characterized the use of reinforced concrete and steel give way to curvilinear and plastic applications of these materials, often inspired by works of civil engineering. In this, whether directly or indirectly, Lautner seems to be responding to many of the preoccupations that engaged architecture between the 1940s and 1990s. This is not to suggest that his work falls in line with the successive twists of the prevailing discourse. On the contrary, his work seems to operate in a strikingly autonomous zone in which the production of his contemporaries is somehow mirrored or refracted from a certain distance, especially in its tones and timing.

This is not so much a matter of influence coming into play as it is a question of Lautner's work exhibiting the mechanisms of intertextuality—the notion in literary theory that common forms and themes can circulate without any explicit points of reference between them.[4] In his own way, Lautner was asking the same key questions that were crossing the minds of a number of architects and engineers who, like himself, were concerned with the tectonics of architecture and with the relationships between building and site, or between structure and the configuration of space.

Like the constructions of Jean Prouvé, the houses of Lautner add up to a sort of menagerie, a collection of characteristic structural solutions based either on wood—whether in solid timbers, plywood, or laminates—or on the vocabulary of concrete in its many delineations. Indeed, Lautner's houses resemble something like a built version of the dictionary of structures proposed by Curt Siegel in 1960.[5] In this way, his built work can be seen as an architecture not of the avant-garde, but, in the sense to which Manfredo Tafuri applied the term, an architecture that is authentically experimental. In comparison with the enquiries of the engineers of his time, which so often resulted in forms that were audacious but uninhabitable, and with the formal experiments of postwar architects, in

Rudolf Schindler, Wolfe House, Avalon, California, 1928–29

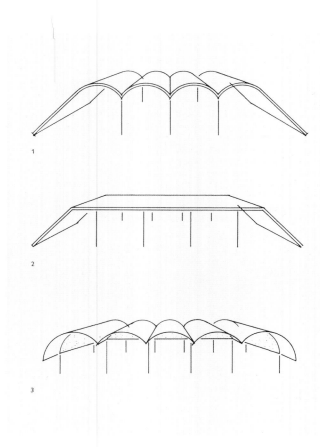

Curt Siegel, schematic drawings from *Impure Shells*, 1960

which the integrity of technical aspects was often disregarded, Lautner saw the necessity of reconciling these different elements of a project.

### GEOGRAPHIES

One could claim that Lautner was among the first to work in the context of a postcolonial space, in which ideas were now starting to move along a south-north axis between Latin America and the United States. With the exhibition *Brazil Builds*, organized by Philip Goodwin with photographs by G. E. Kidder Smith, at the Museum of Modern Art (MoMA) in New York in 1943, a century-long flow of ideas was reversed. Strengthening the already powerful impact of the MoMA catalogue, a spate of special issues of architectural journals on Brazilian modernism was published, and Lautner—opening his practice in the untethered building boom of postwar Los Angeles—could hardly have missed this material.[6] Ten years later came the first extensive presentations of Candela's work in the United States: one of the very first of his articles, "The Shell as a Space Enclosure," appeared in the Southern California review *Arts and Architecture* (to which Lautner himself had been a regular contributor since the 1940s, and whose issues he avidly consumed); along with a major exhibition of his work curated by Esther McCoy at the University of Southern California in 1957.[7]

But the place where his work evolved was also quite simply "Los Angeles," a banal landscape for which he felt nothing but scorn, regarding it much as *Architectural Review* described it in 1950 as "the city un-beautiful par excellence."[8] Nevertheless, the city that Lautner found "so ugly it made me physically sick" simply cannot be understood with conventional aesthetic criteria in mind. Lautner found himself in a region where the innovative technologies of the aerospace and military industries dominated, establishing a culture of innovation that Lautner seems to have taken as a challenge with his own projects. The architectural culture of Los Angeles also stood conspicuously outside the mainstream, by appearing to make every building just one more element in a general spectacle. Taking the two extremes of the "decorated shed" and the "duck" identified by Robert Venturi to characterize this Southern California spectacle, there is no doubt at all that Lautner was making "ducks"; and in doing so he was creating something very different from the architecture that, taking its cues and means from painted wooden scenery, was then studding the city with nostalgic style and modern mannerism. Lautner's long involvement with steeply sloped sites was another position common to Los Angeles architects, whose boldest clients were often—for reasons of economy—compelled to buy the most difficult lots, thereby stimulating the creativity of their designers.[9]

## ANCHORING TO THE GROUND

Many of Lautner's houses appear to rise up from the ground, echoing an idea first formulated by Henry Hobson Richardson and revived by Frank Lloyd Wright from the first Prairie houses onwards. Wright's concern with rooting a building into the ground is particularly apparent in Fallingwater (1934–38), where it is reinforced by the careful siting; while at the Sturges House, which was Lautner's true initiation into architecture in collaboration with Wright, the precarious grace with which it sits on the slope in Brentwood, California, is even more lively than that of Fallingwater at Bear Run, Pennsylvania, which is still firmly attached to the flank of its valley. Indeed, the anchoring line at Sturges is so powerful and bold that one wonders whether Wright—and then Lautner after him—was not aware, at least subliminally, of El Lissitzky's Wolkenbügel concrete project (1923). Looking at certain Lautner dwellings, it is hard not to think of the house at Canoas that Oscar Niemeyer built for himself in Rio de Janeiro in 1953. (Niemeyer loved to tell the story of how Walter Gropius responded to it: "Very good, but impossible to prefabricate."[10]) But there is more in the Canoas House to compare with Lautner than its determination to reach a specific and unique solution: its placement in the valley, surrounded on three sides by jungle and looking out toward the ocean from the other, much like the canyon houses of Los Angeles; the way in which the house is covered by a sinuously contoured concrete slab; and the way it is nestled into the rocks, so that, by using glazed walls and narrow posts, Niemeyer has given the sense that the landscape has been brought inside. Like some of Lautner's houses—the Pearlman Mountain Cabin (1957) comes to mind—it is not so much the building that inhabits the site as the forest that inhabits the building.

## TAKING TO THE AIR

If Lautner knew how to root the building into the earth, he was equally good at dissolving the relationship of house to ground altogether. The Chemosphere (1960), which looks like the hybrid of a flying saucer and a mushroom, seems to belong to the make-believe worlds of 1950s design, and particularly to the widespread inquiry into the freestanding, autonomous home, generally imagined as a circular structure made of new materials, like plastic. The first of these were proposed at the end of the 1920s by R. Buckminster Fuller: his first Dymaxion House was planned, like the Chemosphere, as a polygon, set on a central post, and surrounded with panoramic windows, but held together by cables. It seems quite likely that Lautner, or the client Leonard Malin, who was an aerospace engineer, knew of this project, which had been well circulated in Fuller's publications and in popular illustrated magazines.

*top* El Lissitzky, *Wolkenbügel for Moscow*, 1924, photomontage
*bottom* Oscar Niemeyer, House Niemeyer, Canoas, Rio de Janeiro, Brazil, 1953

*left* John Lautner, Chemosphere, Los Angeles, California, 1960
*above* Richard Buckminster Fuller, Dymaxion House, 1927

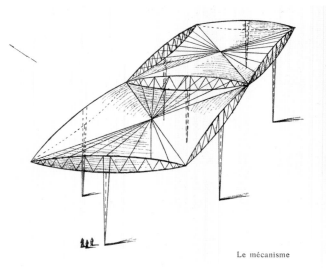

Le mécanisme

top  Jean Prouvé, structure for a spa building, Evian,
France, 1956
above  Le Corbusier, project for the French pavilion,
Exposition de l'Eau de Liège, Belgium, 1937
right  John Lautner, Gantvoort House, Flintridge,
California, 1947

The image of flying saucers, along with real developments in aeronautics and plastics, led many to imagine houses as space containers set on rocks. But Lautner, to whom bubble shapes and sci-fi imagery were alien, was not nearly as concerned with giving a futuristic look to the Malin House as some of his contemporaries were with theirs: Ionel Schein in his plastic house of 1956; the Monsanto House of the Future at Disneyland in 1957; or the cellular forms imagined in the 1960s by "Chaneac" (Jean-Louis Rey) and Pascal Häusermann.

### CARRYING THE ROOF

Though the shell became perhaps the key mode of providing shelter imagined by Lautner, he worked with many other solutions for gaining open space, and for most of these, there are also points of comparison. For the Mauer House he used inverted L-shaped supports similar to those Jean Prouvé imagined ten years later for his pump room at Evian (1956), making the supports in metal rather than wood. The roof of the Gantvoort House (1947) in Flintridge, California, employed lenticular-shaped trusses, for which a precedent can be found in Le Corbusier's 1937 studies for the French Pavilion at the Water Exposition in Liège, Belgium, and which presented the striking image of a great roof floating above its interior spaces. Lautner had probably seen the Le Corbusier design in the Œuvre complete, published in 1947. His own project lacks the complexity of the Frenchman's, but the projects are identical in section.[11] Similarly, the roof of the Carling House brings Niemeyer's Canoas House to mind again, in the way it sets up the fluid relationships of its windowed wall and, more incidentally, in the pattern used for the swimming pool—though it evidently uses a very different support system placed on the outside.

There are many other echoes, some random, that come to mind. The arrangement of the giant trunks of the conifers that carry the circular roof structure at the Pearlman Mountain Cabin is close, perhaps, to that of the pillars that support the Pirovano mountain refuge of Franco Albini at Cervinia, Italy (1951), even though one is carried out in wood and the other in masonry. There are clear affinities between Lautner's Henry's Restaurant in Pomona, California, in 1957 and the Ingalls Rink of Eero Saarinen in New Haven, Connecticut, the design for which, though not built until 1956–58, dates from 1953. They are of different scales and different materials (laminated wood at Pomona and cables at New Haven), and their structural principles are not alike, but they share a similar axial argument and the same vigorous expression of their boundary walls.

## THE LURE OF CONCRETE

Lautner complained constantly about the poor quality of the concrete available to him in Los Angeles, though this was the city that had pioneered developments in this field since the start of the twentieth century, with the building innovations of Irving Gill, Wright, and Schindler.[12] Nevertheless, Lautner's ambitions for concrete remained vast. Indeed, it is striking to note how much reinforced concrete excited the imagination of European and American architects in general, between the start of the 1950s and the end of the 1960s. It was as if this concrete movement had entered its period of decadence. Lautner himself seems to have been hardly interested in the question, raised by the numerous intellectual descendants of Auguste Perret in France and Italy, of the structural skeleton and its expressive possibilities. This issue governed the development of the newly inventive tectonics inspired by Ernesto N. Rogers of the BBPR (Banfi, Belgiojoso, Peressutti and Rogers) office in Italy; and their responses are evident in the Corso Francia building (1959) in Turin, and above all in their famous Torre Velasca (1957), where the armature of the structure is deliberately exposed in counterpoint to the concealed frame of the Pirelli Tower (1956) of Gio Ponti and Nervi. For Lautner, however, it was the inherent character and texture of concrete itself that caught his attention, much as it had captured that of Louis Kahn, who explored it with studied restraint, or Paul Rudolph and I. M. Pei, who did so with much more expressive freedom.[13]

## FOLDING AND MOLDING CONCRETE

Lautner may not have read the philosopher Gilles Deleuze's analysis of the Baroque discovery of the fold, though he certainly knew the mathematics and metaphysics of Gottfried Leibniz in which it was grounded, and used innumerable strategies for bending and folding his surfaces.[14] Some of these workings of the surface into curves come close to those of waveforms or the folds of cloth. Such is the feeling of the roof of the Elrod House (1968), especially when seen from within. Here, it is worth recalling Lautner's strong interest in the Italian design movement of the 1950s. It can be safely assumed that he had become aware, through following that movement, of Italian experiments in undulating form, like those of the Breda Pavilion built by Luciano Baldessari and Marcello Grisotti at the Milan Fair of 1952 and published by Kidder Smith in the following year.[15]

Lautner's most thorough use of the idea of a folded planar surface can be found in the design for the Sheats House (1963), in which the different sections are intensely folded—one upwards and one down. For this, the work of Nervi for the great hall of UNESCO in Paris (1952–60), developed with Marcel Breuer and Bernard Zehrfuss, may have been a source. This idea of the concrete caisson, similar to the way Lautner used it at the Sheats

*left* John Lautner, Pearlman Mountain Cabin, Idyllwild, California, 1957
*above* Franco Albini, Pirovano Sky Lodge, Cervinia, Italy, 1951

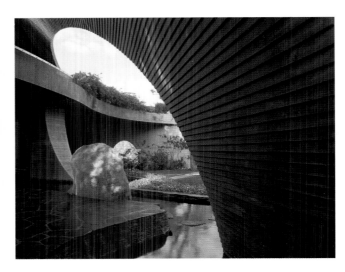

John Lautner, Malibu Cliff House, Malibu, California, 1990

House, also appears in many of Breuer's independent works; but Lautner's triangulation comes closest to the thick ceilings conceived by Louis Kahn for the Yale University Art Gallery (1953), even more than to the geometry of the cupola at Nervi's Palazzetto dello Sport (1958), which Lautner had studied carefully.

### THE LOFTY SHELL

With the large shell, Lautner faced one of architecture's persistent problems—the difficulty of communicating complicated geometric elements in construction drawings or reconciling them with orthodox construction methods. In fact, left to themselves, as in the pavilions of Félix Candela, shell forms, thin and extenuated as they are, simply set up a formal counterpoint to the ground. The lightness of Candela's cabaret La Jacaranda, constructed in Acapulco in 1957, and, even more so, the restaurant Los Manantiales, built the same year in Xochimilco, seems to free them from the ground, as if to reach an almost celestial realm. Lautner's Hope House, though originally based on a shell study by Candela, was finally constructed with a steel roof, and it carries, in contrast to Candela's lightness, a whole sequence of massive volumes that mediates between the great space of its envelope and the ground on which it sits. Saarinen's TWA Terminal (1962) at Idlewild Airport (now John F. Kennedy International Airport) is another exercise in sculptural shell making that did not escape Lautner's attention—and the shadow of its argument falls on many of his projects. At the Garcia House, too, Lautner thought of the shell in terms of its unity with the pillars and the floor slab, placing its main supports at its extremities. Did he perhaps know the extraordinary service station built by Jean-François Zevaco in Marrakesh in 1958? The relationship Zevaco established between the concrete parabola and the stone and concrete blocks that make up its supports conjure up images of similar solutions used by Lautner. Indeed, it is compelling to note that Zevaco, who had been at the École des Beaux-Arts in Paris at the same time Lautner was at Taliesin, and in whose work such lyricism is a central characteristic, had closely observed at the start of his career the buildings of Frank Lloyd Wright, whom he discovered in the 1930s. Many other parallels can be found between the work of this architect, working exclusively in Morocco, and that of Lautner, working almost entirely in California. Like Lautner, Zevaco was fascinated by Niemeyer and by engineers like Torroja and Candela, as can clearly be seen in his market for the rue d'Agadir in Casablanca (1975). And, like Lautner, Zevaco only gave the best of himself to clients with the courage and generosity to experiment with innovations, and the means to realize them in houses of some luxury.[16]

*above* Luciano Baldessari and Marcello Grisotti, Breda Pavilion, Milan Fair, Italy, 1952
*right* Jean-François Zevaco, Gas Station, Marrakesh, Morroco, c. 1958

*above left*  Louis I. Kahn, Yale University Art Gallery, New
Haven, Connecticut, 1969–77: view of the concrete ceiling
*left*  Pier Luigi Nervi with Marcel Breuer and Bernard
Zehrfuss, UNESCO headquarters, Paris, France, 1954–58:
view of folded concrete ceiling
*above*  John Lautner, Sheats House (now Sheats/Goldstein),
Los Angeles, California, 1963

### HETEROGENEOUS STRUCTURES

There is absolutely no dogma in Lautner's attitude to materials; as a result he never subordinates the design concept of his buildings to any rigid rule that would require the primacy of a single material in a project. Even where he demanded rigorous continuity and integrity, as with wood in the Walstrom House and concrete at Mar Brisas and in the initial concept for the Beyer House, he never allowed that to undermine the sense of the structure and always took into account the need for a certain structural logic—though that rational approach to construction is never a synonym for austerity, nor does it stand in opposition to a display of visual richness.

The mixing of solutions did not trouble Lautner. He was happy to bring together steel and concrete (an association almost sacrilegious for some Modernists), as he did in the Desert Hot Springs Motel, where it is difficult not to recognize ideas seen at Taliesin West; to have cables meet concrete and plastic, as in the Tolstoy House; to carry a wooden roof on steel supports, as at the Garcia House; or, so evident in the Chemosphere, to allow three radically different materials to work with each other—a structure of laminated lumber to enclose the dwelling area, metal struts to carry it, those struts bolted into the vertical concrete column that anchors the unit to the hill.

Thus, though they cannot be divorced from the distinctive terrains in which they are grounded, the diversity of Lautner's buildings still presents, if through a refracted lens, the reflection of design ideas developed in pursuit of some very different principles, from the most seemingly neutral technical investigations to the most evidently poetic. At the same time, as the architecture of domestic space seems poised to enter a new cycle of invention— after many years of stagnation—his work has a new relevance, for it manages to free the imagination without abandoning any of its rationality. Far from being—as they have sometimes been portrayed—startling but hollow exercises in architectural sculpture, his houses remain what he intended them to be: spaces in which life is enriched by the unique architectural idea that animates them.

*top left* Félix Candela, La Jacaranda cabaret, Acapulco,
Mexico, 1957
*bottom left* Eero Saarinen, TWA Terminal, Idlewild Airport
(now John F. Kennedy International Airport), New York,
New York, 1956–62
*above* John Lautner, Garcia House, Los Angeles,
California, 1962

John Lautner, Mar Brisas, Acapulco, Mexico, 1973

1 Ziva Freiman, "Interview: John Lautner," *Progressive Architecture*, v. 74, no. 12 (December 1993): 64-67.

2 Le Corbusier, *Toward an Architecture*, trans. John Goodman, intro. Jean-Louis Cohen (Los Angeles: Getty Research Institute for the History of Art and the Humanities, 2007): 98; originally published as *Vers une architecture* (Paris: Crès, 1923).

3 John Lautner, interview by Dominique Lyon, *L'Architecture d'aujourd'hui*, vol. 33, no. 250 (April 1987): 86.

4 Gérard Genette, *Seuils* (Paris: Seuil, 1987) and *Fiction et diction, précédé de Introduction à l'architexte* (Paris: Seuil, 2004).

5 Curt Siegel, *Structure and Form in Modern Architecture* (London: Crosby Lockwood, 1962); originally published as *Strukturformen der modernen Architektur* (Munich: Callwey, 1960).

6 "Architecture of Brazil," *Architectural Record*, vol. 93, no. 1 (January 1943); "Brazil," *Architectural Review*, vol. 95 (March 1944) and vol. 102 (May 1947); *Progressive Architecture*, vol. 28 (April 1947); *Brésil, L'Architecture d'aujourd'hui*, no. 13-14 (1947).

7 Félix Candela, "The Shell as a Space Encloser," *Arts and Architecture*, vol. 72 (January 1955): 12-15; 32-55; Félix Candela, "Stereo-Structures," *Progressive Architecture*, vol. 35 (June 1954): 84-93; "Work of Félix Candela," *Progressive Architecture*, vol. 36 (July 1955): 106-115; Colin Faber, *Candela, the Shell Builder*, with a foreword by Ove Arup (New York: Reinhold Publishing Corp., 1963).

8 "Man Made America," *Architectural Review* 108, no. 648 (December 1950): 362.

9 Frank Escher, ed., *John Lautner, Architect* (London: Artemis, 1994): 283; Dominique Rouillard, "Building the Slope: Hillside Houses 1920–1960," *Arts and Architecture* (1987).

10 Oscar Niemeyer, conversation with Jean-Louis Cohen, Rio de Janeiro, Brazil, 26 January 2000.

11 Max Bill, ed., *Le Corbusier & Pierre Jeanneret Œuvre Complète, 1934–1938* (Zurich: Girsberger, 1947), 172.

12 Harris C. Allen, "The Influence of Concrete on Design in California," *Journal of the American Institute of Architects*, vol. 16 (October 1928).

13 Adrian Forty, "A Material without a History," and Réjean Legault, "The Semantics of Exposed Concrete," in Jean-Louis Cohen, G. Martin Moeller Jr., *Liquid Stone, New Architecture in Concrete* (New York: Princeton Architectural Press, 2006), 54-75; 76-95.

14 Gilles Deleuze, *The Fold: Leibniz and the Baroque* (Minneapolis: University of Minnesota Press, 1993).

15 G. E. Kidder Smith, *Italy Builds: Its Modern Architecture and Native Inheritance* (New York: Reinhold, 1954).

16 Michel Ragon and Henri Tastemain, *Zevaco* (Paris: Cercle d'Art, 1999).

Nicholas Olsberg

# IDEA OF THE REAL

*above* Lake Superior from Midgaard, the Lautner
family house
*page 36* John Lautner in his studio

## A LANDSCAPE OF IDEAS

Along the roads that lead through the North Woods of Wisconsin into Michigan's Upper
Peninsula, there is next to nothing—only tracks to fishing and lumber camps or abandoned
mines. Snow buries this vastness in silence for nearly half the year. The rest of the year
profits from its thawing by a near-audible growth and flux as the climactic seasons drip,
bloom, dry, breed, hum, and freeze again. Lake Superior, here at its midpoint, measures
160 miles to the north and as far to the east and west, while the land on its farther shore
stretches on to the Arctic in a mosaic of low-lying ponds and forests. Quiet as they look,
these remote woods fed Chicago's rage for timber, built the towns of the prairie, laid out
the ties for the railroads, and rendered the iron that built the trestles, the tracks, and the
wheels that moved the country west. Nordic lumbermen and German mining engineers
arrived here, bringing their myths of the forest and a culture that had, for a hundred years,
brooded on the consonance between nature and knowledge, imagination and space,
and upon a Romantic vision of societies constructed to aid the individual quest to grasp
great truths. By the turn of the twentieth century, the peninsula's only city, Marquette, had
therefore become an island of progressive culture, and its liberal institutions had brought
John Lautner's parents there.

His father, also named John Ernest Lautner, had come to Traverse City from
Germany as an immigrant child more than thirty years before. Self-educated, he gained a
place at the University of Michigan as an adult and then studied philosophy in Göttingen,
Leipzig, Geneva, and Paris. In 1901, John Sr., by now equally steeped in the ideas of
German Idealism and the traditions of American Transcendental and Prag-
matic thought, took his first post, as head of French and German at Marquette's North-

ern State Normal School, which had opened two years earlier with thirty-two students and a faculty of six. He soon branched out to teaching and inquiries in the philosophy of society and education.

His mother, Cathleen Gallagher, came from Sheboygan, Wisconsin, at the age of fifteen to look after her sister's children and attend, with them, a new progressive comprehensive school. When they married, in 1907, she was a student at the Normal School and an artist with an interest in Paul Gauguin and the Fauves, in Johann Wolfgang von Goethe's psychological theory of color, in Nordic myths and Sufic and Sanskrit poetry. As her confidence in these interests grew, she adopted the name "Vida" and took as her personal motto the ancient Egyptian symbol of the life force, the *ankh*. By the time John Lautner Jr. was born, on July 16, 1911, the couple had combined these philosophical, metaphysical, and artistic enthusiasms into an entire program for the intellectual, aesthetic, and natural environment in which their two planned children would be raised.

Any account of Lautner must begin, as he always began it, on the shores of Lake Superior, facing a luminous horizon, in a light that stretched to the polar north, among a family who set out willfully to raise a child who would learn from that landscape and from a sympathetic landscape of ideas. To that childhood experience and to the ideas that came out of it, Lautner himself remained impregnably loyal, true to a belief in the observation of nature as a source of learning; to the ideal of a unique 'Idea' governing any work of art; and to faith both in the infinite variety of mind and form and in the possibility of designing that variety into unity. To this was added the 'Realist' notion that truths were embodied in the structuring, shaping, and detailing of things, and from them all came a lifelong confidence in the moral force of the visual imagination, and an immense and practiced sophistication in exercising it. At the same time, Lautner's imaginative and moral thinking defiantly clung to its innocence—one associate called it a "virginal attitude"—and to the innocent ideas that all these truths were discovered through solitary thought and that language was inadequate to express them.[1]

Lake Superior from Midgaard, watercolor by Vida Cathleen Lautner

## THE MIDDLE GROUND

In 1909, Lautner's parents began work on a house in Marquette with the New Jersey architect Joy Wheeler Dow, leader of a reform movement in architecture that he christened the "American Renaissance," as an antidote to the picturesque and medievalizing tastes of the Gilded Age. Based on a seventeenth-century model from Salem, Massachusetts, rendered in raw wood and left without a threshold to meet the ground, Dow's house for the Lautners—self-consciously built as a place reminiscent of the sturdy austerity of the pioneers and as the setting in which "to raise two German Idealist children"—was perhaps the most extreme instance.[2] One visitor even heard the house voice its intent to serve the boy within "by silent example. . . . I will show him my simplicity that he may learn sincerity."[3]

The idea that the home could mold the spirit was a commonplace of the time. But the Lautners took the notion further, turning every element in the form, decoration, space, vistas, plan, and construction of their home into an instrument for "the growth of the soul." Sheltered under a massive, descending Bavarian roof, John and Vida carved and painted the interior in patterns from German, Celtic, Native American, and Nordic folk art, all closely allied to natural rhythms and forms. So Lautner's life began, as it would end, with the belief that a dwelling-place could fertilize the play between space and mind, familiarizing the sublime and sublimating the familiar.

It is hard to imagine anyone whose first home could have been more willfully constructed to place him in the traditions of natural philosophy and Transcendental thought, but the Lautners, with an even firmer didactic intent, went on to construct a second, on a hilltop above the shores of Lake Superior. From 1921 to 1928, working from a library of Norwegian folk architecture guides that Vida gathered, and using rough assembly systems from the lumber and mining industries, the four Lautners (a daughter, Kathleen, was born in 1915) set about designing, constructing, and furnishing—all together and all by hand—a great lodge of logs as a summer cabin. A huge flat rock—celebrated by Lautner as "a billion years old"—crowned the site, and they used this as foundation and deck. John and his father built a dock on the beach below, shipped timbers there, and winched the poles up to the site. John cut the timbers and laid the wooden floor and roof. Sixty years later, in notes for a biographical entry, he remembered "using a windlass for lifting and the most basic of rigging techniques—even resort-

### THE AMERICAN ARCHITECT

which I doubt. They told me, instead, that they were "absolutely delighted" with my efforts to give them what they wanted, and assisted to their utmost afterwards to have the local photographers grasp the ideas sufficiently well to produce these illustrations. Probably there is not a professional photographer in Marquette who has ever read "The Scarlet Letter," and anyway he would not have understood what "The Scarlet Letter" had to do with his taking a picture of a very distinctive, up-to-date house.

It is not the same, you know. Nobody asked Germany for her [deleted] kultur. It was entirely unsolicited; whereas, when you come to an architect you come as you do to a physician, in quest of pro-

LIVING ROOM, "KEEPSAKE," MARQUETTE, MICH.

fessional assistance. You may tell him you want chocolate bonbons in lieu of medicine; but he knows, and you know, that first, last and always, you want your health, and to that end you pay him for his skill, *not* his affections. Then people who think I can help them are usually a long way from the abecedarian class. Rarely does it happen in practice as it did to me once at a card party where a fascinating *ingenue* across the table, to whom I was explaining that five tricks scored two points in euchre, interrupted to inquire, naively: "Mr. Dow, what *are* tricks?"

Rarely have I to explain the difference between a cornice and a water-table. If I do have to explain that without the dramatic story and historic atmosphere we build the house in vain—we build anything in vain. There are less impatient teachers than myself for the primary grades. It is the fourth dimension of architecture that the pupils take up in my room. Only don't think by that I refer to any mathematical contortion—a last spasm of the human mind before losing its equilibrium. Nothing

of the kind. It is the element of personality, of spirituality and companionship which may be embodied in an architectural design. "Keepsake" stands for this legitimate fourth dimension, for it is teeming with legends, memoirs and personalities. You don't have to send out for company; the folks

FIREPLACE IN COTTAGE AT MARQUETTE, MICH.

are already there. We may play in it the edifying game of "Let's pretend" over again with all the zest of childhood; and away down deep who is not a "Sentimental Tommy" as soon as someone happens to strike the responsive chord? You may have missed it in music. There is a nocturne by Frederic Chopin you have not heard. It is some cunningly pointed gable up in New England, in combination with a great, clustered chimney about which owls and elfin moonlight play—that finally gets you on the wire.

The Charles II gables of "Keepsake" are lopsided gables. The rafters across the front pitch at different angle from that of those extending to the low eaves at the rear. The latter are a little less

DINING TABLE RECESS IN LIVING ROOM—COTTAGE AT MARQUETTE, MICH.

*left* "Keepsake," Lautner House, Marquette, Michigan, 1912, designed with Joy Wheeler Dow, from *American Architect*, May 28, 1918

*above* Midgaard under construction, c. 1925, with the young John Lautner seated at the shore and working on the roof

## HOME BUILDING

# Midgaard

## A Norse Cabin
## on
## Lake Superior

BY

VIDA CATHLEEN LAUTNER

Interior view of Midgaard, from "'Midgaard,' a Norse Cabin on Lake Superior," by Vida Cathleen Lautner, *Home Building*, June 1927

ing to the necessity of sighting the horizon to obtain a level—to construct it." This exercise, he added, taught him all his "fundamental lessons in architecture."

Every summer, from 1924 to 1928, students were hired to work with the family on the summer house, and the long days together were filled with conversations on philosophy, anthropology, education reform, and the nature of civil society. In John Sr.'s thinking, a quest for 'integrity' was foremost—the search to discover social processes that could reconcile the ideal of community with the absolute independence of the individual, the Whitmanesque vision of America as a kind of molecular society. Then came faith in that individualism, which father and son both defined, in its rich old-fashioned meaning, as 'common sense'—the Romantic premise that everyone has access to an inner grasp of universal truths, developed from "mute observation," "from the within," and in sympathy with nature. Along with these ideas from Immanuel Kant, Thomas Carlyle, and Friedrich Nietzsche, Lautner's father passed on to his son the core points in the aesthetics of George Santayana, with whom he studied briefly at Harvard. Santayana argued that 'beauty' lies in the work of art that exercises reason to reconcile man with his environment, and that such artistic ideas can only grow out of the play between how we sense the external world and what those sensations breed in the unconscious. The Lautners called this mix of ideas 'Realism.' This was the term Hegel had used to express the process through which the apparent disorder of Nature and the evident banality of the everyday were rendered into a sublime structure by the application of mind and idea. Young Lautner carried the antirationalist implications of this philosophy further. He came to believe in instinctive procedures as the only means to locate an authentic logic for design, and in the innate 'vitality' of the inanimate things thus made. This resulted in a very American sense of things and spaces being alive to something more than their history or habitation, the feeling famously identified by Nathaniel Hawthorne that there can be sites, scenes, and buildings where the real and the imagined meet, and each—the human mind and the fabricated world—adopt the nature of the other.[4]

These were ideas fundamental to Lautner's thinking as an architect. But Lautner's near-mystical passion for the cabin on the lake also suggests how powerful and lasting the eclectic metaphysics of his mother were. As the cabin—a single open space with a high, surrounding mezzanine for sleeping—neared completion, Vida directed the family in carving and painting its decorations, inscribing a helix, wheel, and circle—symbols of the sun, the heavens, and their cycles. And then, Vida wrote, "The sunset over the Huron Mountains, with its path across the lake, and the feeling we get, when on our balconies, of being connected with the heavens, inspired us to name the cabin 'Midgaard' . . . midway between earth and heaven."[5] The word *midgaard*, in Nordic legends, stands not just for the space between earth and sky, but also for the bridge between the describable phenomena of earthly knowledge and the indefinable knowledge of the heavens. It is an idea akin to the great lodges of the native peoples of the Lake Superior shore, in which architecture shapes a meeting ground between the earth and sky; it is evident in what Lautner's father felt

*below left* Bench at Midgaard
*below right* Ceiling at Midgaard

when he wrote of the peculiar force that appears wherever the power of the wilderness meets the strength of what mankind engineers to tame it; it is what the young Lautner had in mind when, in 1932, he raised and rebuilt the roof at Midgaard on a heroic scale, and had his mother paint a sky upon its timbers; and it is what, step by step in his long career, Lautner saw as the first function of architecture—to build the space between.

### IDEAS INTO ARCHITECTURE, 1933-1938

Lautner entered the liberal arts program of the Northern State Teachers College (formerly the Normal School)—now a full-fledged state college—in 1929. Here, he followed a curriculum of philosophy, ethics, physics, literature, drafting, art, and architectural history. He played woodwinds and piano, discovered jazz, looked at new art, and traveled with his father to the Southwest on anthropological surveys. Lecture and reading notes show him studying Bergson on perception, Kant on instinct, and Henri Frederic Amiel's *Journal Intime* on the autonomy of inspiration; and reflecting on the 'Modern' as a search for something "as free and pure as sunlight." At the same time, he discovered that he had absolutely no talent for the measured drawing, and that he distrusted analysis, explanation, and the power of words. As a result—although determined to become an architect—he rejected the idea of any formal course of study.

Responding to what she saw as his uncertainty, but acknowledging his intoxication with modern tendencies in all the arts, Lautner's mother, in April 1933, turned to Frank Lloyd Wright, who had opened an apprenticeship program six months earlier at Taliesin, his home in Spring Green, Wisconsin. Lautner was quickly admitted to the new Taliesin Fellowship, but there were two obstacles: he had become engaged to one of his neighbors, Mary "Marybud" Roberts, and he could not afford the fee. Vida Lautner appealed to Marybud's mother, Abby Beecher Roberts, suggesting that the young couple enroll together,

and that Marybud's mother pledge the fees for both. Persuaded by a visit to Spring
Green, Roberts complied. Lautner at once saw the danger that Wright's astonishing com-
mand of design might have on the formation of his own approach, avoiding the drafting
room and delighting, as his fellow apprentices recall and as he told Mrs. Wright at the end
of their lives, in the daily work of "carpenter, plumber, farmer, cook, and dishwasher, that is,
as an apprentice, which I still believe is the real way to learn the requirements of architecture." Clearly a favorite and a leader, he filled in for Wright in weekly talks at Unity Chapel,
toured visitors, wrote about projects and ideas for the Madison press, and gathered
students around him for debate.

    Lautner's background, rooted in a quest for a decisively American, individualist,
and anticommercial society, made him already sympathetic to Wright's thinking. Before
he settled at Taliesin, he copied and starred two aphorisms from the end sheets of
Wright's *Modern Architecture*, published in 1931. First was the attack on superficial
effect that Wright made in his distinction between "the *curious* and the *beautiful*,"
one resulting from the imposition of imagination onto a work of architecture, and the
other arising from the imaginative logic of an idea developed from the setting or
situation. The second idea was simpler: "Individuality is sacred—Let us dedicate this
republic to multiply and elevate that quality in all art and architecture." Even more
ready than Wright to see himself as a beleaguered upholder of truths to which others
were blind, Lautner himself railed against the superficial state of a greedy and fame-
driven society, writing for a 1935 Taliesin talk of America as a "shopkeeper society"—
a materialist and speculator culture that was incapable of "living in the realm of ideas."
In June 1936 he delivered a more complex assault on mass production, mass mar-
keting, and mass society, seeing its specialization of tasks as divisive, separating men
from one another and alienating them from nature. Asking how to revive a common
life when each part has lost a sense of the whole, he answered that only an individual
focus on inner truth, a quest to be whole in oneself, can produce a genuine community or a reconciliation with the natural world. This approach to individualism is what
drove his work for the rest of his life. Singular works of architecture—perfectly
sited, variously formed, and ignoring rhetorical distinctions between public and private so that every space inhabited becomes one to own—would
be for him the building blocks of a true society.

    His working association with Wright went on for at least eleven years, gradually
moving from apprenticeship to loose collaboration, and finally ending when he had
established his independent practice in 1947. At Taliesin he designed little from scratch
except for a tentlike dwelling at the Arizona camp (which began his long inquiry into roof

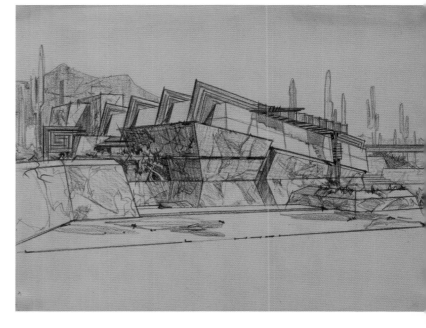

*left* Lautner's tent, Taliesin West, Scottsdale, Arizona, 1937
*above* Frank Lloyd Wright, Taliesin West Drafting Room,
Scottsdale, Arizona, c. 1941: study sketch found in Lautner's
personal papers

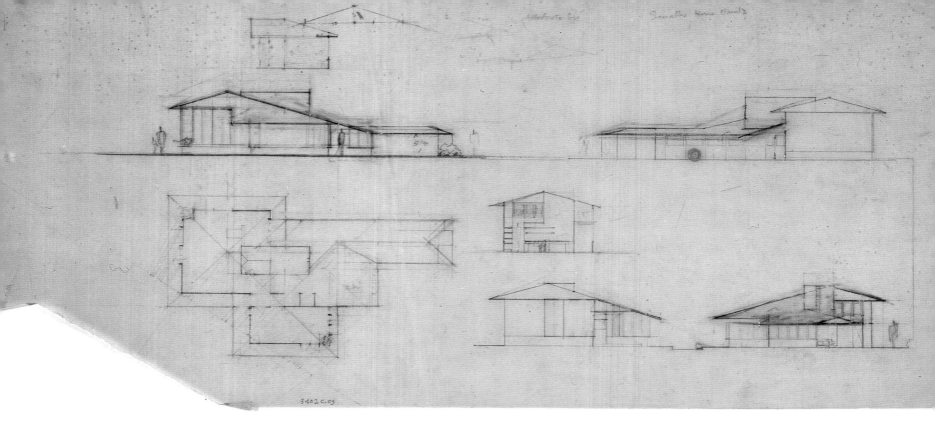

Frank Lloyd Wright, Taliesin Fellowship Small House
Projects, 1934: plan and elevations, drafted by John Lautner

structures). But by 1934, he was designing construction details for a small house for Alice
Millard in Los Angeles and for the Playhouse and Studios at Taliesin. A year later he was
assigned to what would become a two-year task to supervise the house in Marquette for
Marybud's mother. In 1937, he agreed to oversee Wingspread, the vast villa complex for
Herbert Johnson near the Lake Michigan shore north of Racine, Wisconsin, developing
many of Wingspread's structural systems and details and watching the Johnson Wax Administration Center (1936) emerge two miles away. He wrote with excitement about how
Johnson Wax's mushroom posts floated "a roof to sandwich life between earth and sky"
and opened up its interior space. He traveled with Wright to direct photography at the
Willey House in Minneapolis, Minnesota (1934). With its rising roofline, contradictory abut-
ment to the lot, and flow between its living room and garden terrace, this house became a
critical source for his own small houses. While Taliesin West (1938) emerged, he became
deeply involved with the construction of its Drafting Room, later filming the angled roof
trusses, which reached to the ground, and drawing on them for his Mauer House (1946).
Though strikingly original from the start, Lautner's work is not, therefore, completely independent of the "influence" he so dreaded.

Wright's Roberts House (1936) was based on Lautner's design for a small house
for the Broadacre City project, and it was as near as Lautner came to a work of his own at
Taliesin. He explained his Broadacre house model as "plastic," with "windows from floor
to ceiling across the entire living room," arguing that because "Nature is plastic . . . it fit
perfectly—it looked at the view, it grew out of the site, it was spacious yet small enough for
two." The Roberts House adjusted this design to a sloping site, dramatically tilting its living
room roof up to the sky. Lautner described it in phenomenological terms, beginning and
ending with the site: "The Roberts House projects itself out of a sand hill, looking over
other low hills crowned with cedars to Lake Superior beyond. . . . The living room roof and
ceiling pitches up, like one's eyelash under a visor to the sky, leaving nothing but glass
between you and the view. . . . At night you see the moon and stars instead of the walls of

the room. . . . In the morning the sun comes all the way to the heart of the house to wake
you. . . . The house unfolds out of the hills into a rhythmic, light, free space. . . ."

The Roberts House—extending space through obtuse angles, tilting its roof, and
rotating interlocking rectangles in the plan—would become central to Lautner's strategy
for siting and shaping small houses. Wingspread's influence was less direct, but Lautner
must have retained a powerful memory of the months spent setting Wingspread's vast
cart-wheeling *parti* onto, over, and under the quiet undulations of the site. Wingspread
shows its sympathy for the terrain not by deferring to its slight rise and fall,
but by setting up a counterpoint to it, radiating on a single plane that drama-
tizes the slight shifts of the prairie landscape beneath, making nature, as Lautner
and Wright so boldly claimed, "*more* significant and beautiful."

It was an astonishing time to be with Wright; in the years before 1936, Wright's
contact with his apprentices was almost constant, and he
introduced them to his European visitors—Erich Mendelsohn,
Paul Frankl, H. T. Wijdeveld, J.J.P. Oud, Mies van de Rohe,
and others. Work and conversation moved far beyond the
conventional boundaries of "architecture." For the first two
years, Wright gave illustrated talks every Tuesday night and
lectures on Sundays. He talked of the interdependence of
structure and space, analyzed the third dimension in the
Japanese print, introduced his own unbuilt projects of the
1920s—notably the Lake Tahoe resort, the Doheny Ranch
Resort, and most significantly for Lautner the spiraling concrete Automobile Objective for Gordon Strong. Students
went to Madison to hear Walter Gropius and Le Corbusier,
and as the winter visits to Arizona began in 1935, spent
nights at the Wright sites en route. In March 1935, a three-
day lecture tour with Wright of his Los Angeles work imbued
them all with "the gospel of concrete"; a pilgrimage was
made to see the concrete curve of the Hoover Dam; and
Lautner's personal acquaintance with Wright's work deep-
ened as he assembled photography for a 1938 special
issue of *Architectural Forum* and returned to Taliesin to help
with models and materials for a 1940 Museum of Modern
Art exhibition.

Lautner making a model of the Abby Beecher Roberts
House (Deertrack) for Wright's Broadacre City exhibition for
Radio City Music Hall, New York, 1935

Lautner brought to his discussions with Wright his own well-formed views, influenced by Kant and Bergson. "The intellect is not infallible," Lautner argued in his first talk to the Fellowship in May 1934, "Instead, it is only a tool of instinct . . . and the deeper sense called intuition."[1] Only instinctive processes could bring about "the feeling of growth from the ground up" to which every building must aspire. A few weeks later, in a debate on painting Lautner argued that no work of art is complete in itself because "the whole environment enters into the observer to alter the picture."[2] This sense of the substantial being transformed by the ineffable, and the nature of the object determined by its surroundings, is close to Santayana's expansive view of aesthetic perception, which drew the visceral and ethereal together. But it borrowed too from Vida's readings of eastern mystics, from whom she drew the idea that any object of beauty brought alongside it, like a mandala, the invisible universe it walked beside.

Yet Lautner's and Wright's paths diverged. Whereas Wright remained cautious, even afraid, of his own exuberance, Lautner was more ready to risk its embrace. Lautner also dwelt, as Wright never did, on the idea of permanence and solidity. He saw buildings as containers for change, writing in notes at Taliesin the sequential formula that governed his last works: "integrity—vitality—immortality." From the Harvey House (1950) onwards, Lautner became increasingly obsessed with durability. Wright, on the other hand, was almost recklessly inclined to let one building go as he moved on to the next, and to test new materials with little regard for their sustainability. Above all, Wright assembled a whole, guided by his pencil, a grid, and modules but Lautner saw from the start a complete vaulting shape and space, or an interlocking set of them, and sensed its structure and its connections to the space around. However total the vision that prompted a Wright design, it was essentially always a composition. Lautner, instead, seems to have begun with a new shape or form, full-blown and overarching, in his mind. Wright, radically and brilliantly, thought like an architect, Lautner like a sculptor or a potter at the wheel, to whom, even as a convenience, a gridded sheet of paper, a modular geometry, or even a pencil were without utility.

## THE SMALL HOUSE PROBLEM IN AMERICA

"Architecture," Wright said to his students in 1934, "begins and ends with the . . . small compact house with a modern sense of space."[1] That proposition consumed Taliesin for the years of Lautner's residency, dominated his working relationship with Wright in the four years that followed, and would occupy the bulk of his creative energies until the end of the 1940s. Like the Lautners, Wright had always seen the dwelling as a space for the "growth of the soul," and the middle-class home as the primary architectural instrument to

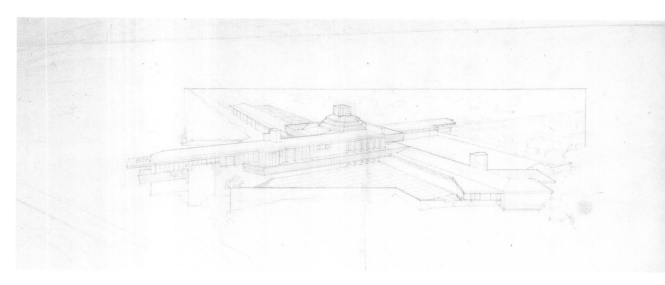

*left* Frank Lloyd Wright, Johnson Wax Administration Center, Racine, Wisconsin, 1936: view of the interior
*above* Frank Lloyd Wright, Wingspread, Wind Point, Wisconsin, 1937: study, perspective

reform society. By 1919, as industry spread, as the automobile became available to blue-collar households, and as the economic condition of America's working families approached the managerial class, Wright now saw the working-class house and the increasingly divided structure of the burgeoning city as the two most urgent fields for new thinking. In the wake of the Depression and with the New Deal's promise of large-scale reconstruction, Wright began to consolidate this thinking into inquiries at a new scale, a scale that looked to a greatly dispersed urban fabric and was loosely presented to the Fellowship and the world as Broadacre City.

An intensive study of the small house, conducted by the apprentices, followed and was published by the Fellowship at the end of 1934. At about the same time, Edgar Kaufmann, the Pittsburgh department store baron, visited and suddenly turned this scheme from an inquiry into a proposition. Seeing it as a spur for the New Deal reconstruction program, Kaufmann sponsored the fabrication of a set of models and plans, and arranged a national tour of these schemes to open in New York in April 1935. At the end of the exhibition's tour, Lautner's and Marybud's parents arranged for the young couple to install and present the exhibition in Marquette. Lautner adapted the exhibition to center not on the general scheme of a dispersed city but on large-scale models of Broadacre Houses—minimum and middle-class zoned dwellings "designed with large-scale prefabrication in mind . . . [and] a convenient unit system" that allowed for "variety without repetition."[2] Lautner described the aspiration of these house designs in personal notes for a Broadacre farm dwelling as "one large sheltered space with a sense of freedom . . . suitable to growth and change . . . inside and out . . . a *productive* building for *creative* living." Broadacre was attempting to establish a new and very American sense of community—the "Democratic Vista" envisaged by Walt Whitman—by dispersing the city into the natural world. Lautner seized upon this idea. In a letter akin to a manifesto, he told Wright that "the nature of human nature as *of* nature opens new vistas . . . a new unity and coherence in

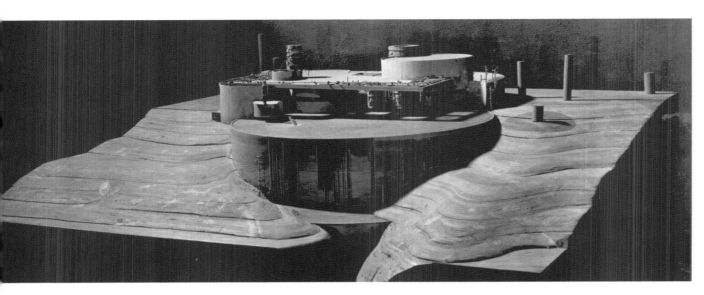

Frank Lloyd Wright, Jester house project, Palos Verdes, California, 1938: model

everything!" The Broadacre ideal with many of its specific models for the new city—its minimum and repeatable independent housing units along with service stations and highway markets—informed Lautner's wartime studies of mass housing, his roadside and small house experiments of the 1940s and 1950s, and mature projects such as the Chemosphere (1960), the Stevens House (1968), and the vast Alto Capistrano project (1963–1969). As late as 1991, Lautner continued to look to Broadacre as a possible future. What most intrigued him was the Broadacre idea that "new patterns of living" could be opened to all classes simply by taking its doctrine of decentralization into all spheres and scales—opening up domestic spaces, humanizing the feeling of social spaces, and changing the relationship between built and open spaces. With this in mind, Lautner quit the Fellowship in 1938 and moved to Los Angeles to build these "houses for decentral-ized life." To look at all the work that followed—however flamboyant, luxurious, or radically structured and sited—we must keep in mind this moral stance: Lautner's designs attempt to change the patterns of everyday life to make a society and culture more aware of its surroundings and their commonality.

The immediate terms of Lautner's departure from Taliesin are cloudy, but the proxi-mate cause is clear: Marybud was pregnant. It was time to move out and to make a living. Lautner arrived in Los Angeles in March 1938. He told Wright that although seeking an independent career, he remained "ready to do anything you or the Fellowship need." Two ambitious Los Angeles projects by Wright were then in development: one-hundred system-atized "All-Steel" sheet-metal houses designed as a walkable garden suburb for Baldwin Hills, in which all structure, facades, details, appliances, and furnishings used metal posts, sheets, and beams; and the series of circular bent plywood drums known as the Jester house project, for Palos Verdes. Both—in their treatment of the slope and in their radical formal and spatial thinking—resonate powerfully with Lautner's independent work of the next ten years. But Lautner, using Marybud's pregnancy as an excuse—their daughter, Karol, was born May 30, 1938—did little for Taliesin for the next months, and the projects were dead before the end of the year. In fact, under an agreement with his contractor friend Paul Speer, "who will give me $100 per house," Lautner was trying his own hand in the low-cost housing field. A one-bedroom frame house for the Springer family, designed in 1938 and built for $2,500, was the first, and possibly only, fruit of this collaboration.

With little scope for formal experiment, except for a rising roof and angled cross-beams, Lautner focused on the detail and palette, exposing the frame and painting it in red iron oxide, hanging tan canvas ceilings, and using rough tan plaster on the walls.

The Springer House (1940) was published almost as soon as it appeared, but it brought little in the way of new commissioned work. Lautner spent most of 1938 drawing on his Taliesin inquiries into low-cost housing to develop ideas for prefabricated plywood houses, designing a model trailer, and writing papers that addressed the emerging housing crisis in Southern California—the pressure of an expanding aircraft industry and the arrival of Dust Bowl migrants were beginning to stretch existing dwelling stock to its limits. Early in September 1938, Wright wrote to say that, so long as Lautner saw "some asset to himself" as he tried to get his practice started, Wright would be happy to revive their working relationship, and he proposed they focus on a flexible system for a Southern California version of the "modest home." Two weeks later they agreed to work together, and over the next months five small Los Angeles house projects emerged—for the Sturgeses, Lowes, Greens, Bells, and Mauers. A sixth, the small house for Alice Millard on which Lautner had worked in 1934, reappeared briefly in 1941. Early in 1941, when two other Los Angeles projects ran into trouble—the redesign of the Ennis House and the construction of a palatial complex for Arch Oboler in the Malibu Hills—Lautner was engaged to repair the damage. In 1942, yet another California project, for additions to a farm complex for the Astor family in the desert near Indio, came to Wright. With the Fellowship emptied by conscription, Wright essentially consigned the Astor design to Lautner, supervising his plans.

Thus, though their work together was checkered and sporadic, Lautner remained associated with Wright, working on as many as eleven projects altogether, throughout his first five years in California. Indeed, Lautner, more than any of the other talents who went through Wright's stable, retained his association with Wright for longer, and on terms that were more trusting, less jealous, and more independent. One can argue that

Frank Lloyd Wright, Bell house project, Los Angeles, California, 1939: presentation drawing, perspective

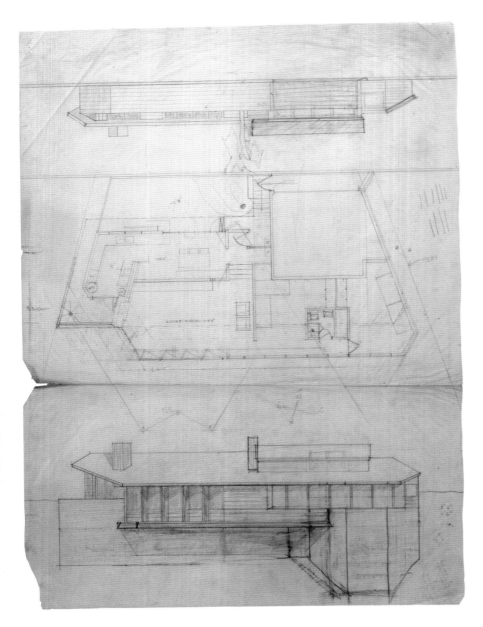

Lautner House, Los Angeles, California, 1940: study, plan and elevations

Lautner was Wright's true successor, and that Wright saw him as such—Lautner kept American architecture alive to the Romantic tradition to which both were heirs, he fit Wright's thinking to new economies of structure and to a changing society, and he reached for a sculptural freedom and a psychic intensity that took Wright's principles into exuberant new territory.

George and Selma Sturges had asked Wright for a small house with a view. Their site search ended with a forty-five-degree sloped lot in Brentwood, which Lautner declared perfect, fraught with possibilities for terraces and vistas. Wright proposed a wooden structure using the modular, structural, and spatial thinking behind the Taliesin small house studies and the just-finished Jacobs House (1936) in Madison, Wisconsin—"as an authentic unit in the low-cost housing field."[3] Sketches came from Wright in February 1939 for a tiny free-plan house, set on a spacious terrace that cantilevered dramatically over the sheer hillside beneath it—"one of the simplest things we have done and one of the best."[4] In June, Wright came out to work on it with Lautner and to discuss the plans for the Bell, Green, Mauer, and Lowe houses. By the end of August, Lautner received construction drawings, hired Paul Speer to contract the job, and began to obtain permits.

Things quickly started going wrong. Lautner had agreed to add steel supports to allay the city's fears about the canti-lever, and the Sturgeses' engineer then studded the scheme with steel beams and posts, and the costs of the project soared from $6,000 to $11,000. Wright believed the house had been ruined by thus "divorcing the structure from the design . . . the building is now all cut up and cut off—hanging to a skeleton."[5] With the Sturgeses' interest payments now totaling more than half the cost of construction, Lautner tried to hurry the project. He raced to finish full construction details when site work was nearly completed, and he built and finished the whole structure in the two disastrously wet months of November and December. By the end of the Sturgeses' first year in the house, materials and joints were failing. Ready to move out and sue for the funds necessary to make the house sellable, they blamed Lautner: "John is not a great overseer! Money does not exist for him," said George, noting that his arrogance on site led him to substitute "offensive witticisms" for reasonable cautions and corrections.[6] Lautner worked on corrections slowly through much of 1941, still not to the Sturgeses' satisfaction. In March 1942, Wright himself completed repairs by bringing in students from Taliesin.

A few years earlier, in 1938, at about the same time the Sturgeses' plans developed, Lautner bought land in Silver Lake for a small house project of his own, a "monomaterial" study in unfinished redwood boards. In deliberate contrast to the Sturges House, which was a tiny rectangular platform floating like a birdcage over a steep slope on an expansive brick perch, Lautner slipped his own house under the street line and into the slope with far greater economy. He tried "to build something of the hill rather than in spite of the hill. . . . The angularity of the house was due not only to the lot lines, but also to my desire for a warmth, casualness, and continuity contributing to a sense of greater space. The angles had to be carried through for greater unity—a particularly important point in a small house. And they also give that feeling of freedom which American architecture should have." Henry-Russell Hitchcock favorably contrasted it with other contemporary wooden houses built on similar sites, preferring it to the theatrical siting of Wright's Sturges House or the complicated play of planes used by Harwell Harris: "less of a virtuoso performance than Wright's . . . and simple in plan and economical in execution as Wright has rarely had occasion to be. . . . Lautner uses diagonals more cleanly and less arbitrarily than Harris and has for wooden construction an advancing rather than a semi-traditional feeling."[7] Wright, visiting in June 1939, carefully compared it to Schindler's wooden dwellings and found it "much closer to the root."[8] The house was an immediate popular success. *House Beautiful*, treating it as a do-it-yourself model home, published both an article and a handbook of plans and specifications.

By the time the Lautners moved into their house in the summer of 1939, they were already preparing to move out. Lautner disliked the flashy money-driven city, describing "life and work out here" as "too rotten to imagine," and attributing the ill health he suffered in his first year there to a revolt against its "indescribable ugliness." Lautner was considering a move to either Rio de Janeiro or Boston—or returning to Taliesin. Wright came out to work with him in September 1939, inviting him back to Taliesin West for the winter season. The Lautners went to Arizona to rejoin the Fellowship, working with Wright on the Bell and Green houses and on models and plans for Wright's retrospective at the Museum of Modern Art. But by the end of April

Frank Lloyd Wright with John Lautner, Sturges House, Los Angeles, California, 1939: model

*above* "House Against the Horizon"—Bell House, Los
Angeles, California, 1940
*right* Bell House, Los Angeles, California, 1940: view
of interior

Frank Lloyd Wright, Eaglefeather project, Malibu, California, 1941: study, perspective

1940, Lautner had decided to remain "on my own resources" and returned to Los Angeles to "package small houses." The permits for Wright's Bell House were issued in June, but both the Bell and Green projects slowly stalled as costs surpassed their budgets. The Greens simply canceled, but Wright gave the Bell commission to Lautner, with the generous comment that perhaps Lautner could give them more for their money. Designs for the Mauer House began that fall, but when Wright failed to finish working drawings in time for the clients to keep their loan, the Mauers dropped Wright and turned to Lautner. Lautner excused this "monkey business" by saying that neither he nor Wright could progress in the small house field unless they had concrete examples to show clients that were desirable, economical, and viable.

As it turned out, Lautner would not complete the Mauer House for another five years, but his version of the Bell House moved quickly into construction. Lautner essentially took the plan that Wright had developed for the Greens and adapted it to the site and the clients' needs, focusing on an angled projection out to a terrace against the horizon, breaking up the light, and emphasizing the form with a vertical wooden screen. On a limited budget, the idea, as he described it, was to "beautify the basic" by "capturing the sun" and extending its flow toward terrace and vista to gain a sense of "spaciousness beyond its dimensions." The house was a publicity triumph. As the national preoccupation with the postwar house began, it appeared in a three-page spread in *Arts and Architecture* in June 1942, titled "House against the Horizon."[9] In the May 1944 issue, *House and Garden* announced it as the model house for California living; the University of Chicago solicited plans and drawings of the house as a studio teaching tool; in 1947, the inaugural issue of the avant-garde *California Designs* presented the Bell and Mauer houses as the anchoring points for a discussion of the "California Theory" that "the disorganized" and a "lack of regimentation" were giving "a new slant to the American way of life"; from 1946 to 1947, it appeared with critical comment in *Architectural Forum* and *Progressive Architecture*; and in *The Californian* in 1948 as a model for the new suburb.[10]

Meanwhile, Wright's Eaglefeather (1941)—a hilltop Malibu extravaganza for the filmmaker Arch Oboler—was running into trouble. Lloyd Wright, Frank Lloyd Wright's son, oversaw construction drawings and supervision, but Lloyd was fired by Oboler in March 1941. Wright came to Los Angeles and arranged for Lautner to complete the project under an independent contract with the client. Thus commenced an impossibly entangled saga, which ended with the construction of a gatehouse, walls, guest quarters, and a "retreat" for Oboler's wife, Eleanor. In September 1941, as elements of the composition began to appear, Wright visited. He complained that Lautner had allowed costs to get out of hand; objected to the Alvar Aalto furniture that Lautner had introduced, lecturing Lautner on the dishonesty of Aalto's use of a rigid material (wood) to imitate the sprung behavior of a flexible one (wire coils); and condemned Lautner's concessions to Oboler in siting. Wright's apprentices invaded the site in March 1942 and demolished the offending walls without Oboler's consent. Lawsuits followed, and Lautner returned to Taliesin for yet another sojourn to resolve the disputes. Lautner and Wright weathered the storm well, attributing their difficulties with Oboler to the "viciousness of Flicker Town." By the end of 1942, wartime constraints ended this ravishing piece of mountaintop architectural theater. But for Eleanor's retreat, Lautner designed elements that carried into his work of the 1940s. Both there and in the unrealized main house are kernels of Wright's thinking that ripened dramatically in Lautner's own: shaping the object to the horizon, radiating structure into landscape, setting the topography itself in relief, and—as at the Sturges House before it or Silvertop and Chemosphere after—floating living space into a territory somewhere between earth and sky.

Exempt from the military draft, but unable to build, Lautner now harked back to the Broadacre dream, and decided again to leave Los Angeles. From the summer of 1942 through 1944, Lautner fruitlessly sought work with local planning commissions, regional plan associations, and reconstruction agencies all over the United States and Canada. Desperate, he took a job, through Paul Speer, with the Structon Company. He planned and supervised building for the U.S. Army Corps of Engineers at the airport in Bishop, California, and for defense-related community services nearby, including

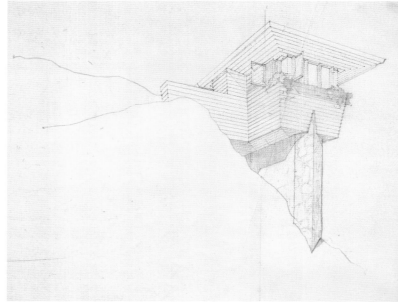

Frank Lloyd Wright, Eleanor's Retreat at Eaglefeather, Malibu, California, 1941–42: study, perspective

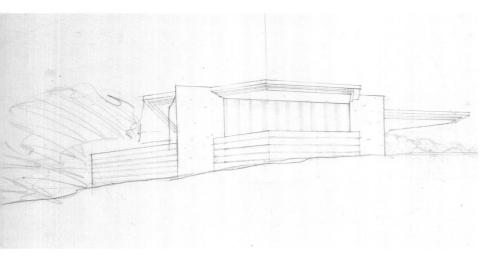

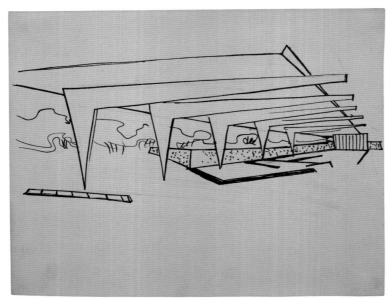

top Frank Lloyd Wright, Mauer House, Los Angeles,
California, 1939: study, perspective
bottom John Lautner, Mauer House, Los Angeles,
California, 1946: sketch, perspective of roof structure

a school and a clinic. Structon was adapting to the demand for faster construction by exploring prefabricated panel systems in many materials—concrete included. In the year or more he worked for the company, Lautner vastly expanded his knowledge of engineering and construction, his material dreams, and his structural imagination. At the same time, he became determined to offset "the monotony of standardiza-tion" that typically came from rapid construction systems. Leaving Structon sometime in 1944, Lautner set to work on new ideas for systematized building with the small house and the Broadacre ideal once more foremost in his mind. That summer he worked with Whitney Smith on a "research house" for fifty-by-fifty-foot lots, reworking Smith's plans and struc-tural system to achieve "even more flexibility and continuous spaces." At the same time, he returned to his 1938 studies for prefabricated plywood houses and trailer homes. These he merged into a single variable "nomad house," a ready-cut mobile assembly that he called "a smooth, flexible camp frag-ment" out of which an instant city, responsive to the migra-tions that marked these years, could rise. Toward the end of 1945, he partnered with the architect Samuel Reisbord to develop a twenty-acre tract of prefabricated, single-fam-ily houses. Drawings for this unrealized scheme are lost, but Lautner wrote that he worked strenuously to draw out from standard components "a maximum variation of design," and—as at the Springer cottage—to intensify the variety and the vigor of the whole through "textures, colors, contrast."

As the war ended, Lautner joined the firm of the flourishing society architect Douglas Honnold as design associate. The work produced with Lautner as design principal was rapidly recognized, earning them notice in *Progressive Architecture*, *Arts and Archi-tecture*, and *Architectural Forum*; the Southern California American Institute of Architects (AIA) award in 1946 for the outstanding body of work in 1945; and a special AIA award for five years' achievement in 1947. Despite this fruitful collaboration, Lautner's letterhead continued to show him in sole practice and with an independent business address. And it was as sole architect that he took up the war-delayed project, inherited from Wright, for a $6,000 house for the Mauers.

The Mauer House is perhaps the first research study in the single-family postwar California dwelling to have risen from the ground. It addressed the same opportunity as the Case Study Houses: a million veterans moving into the Southern California sunshine with young families to raise, G.I. loans in their pockets, and a pledge from their president of their own hygienic house as the reward for three brutal years of service. As Raymond Kappe notes, Lautner shared with his friends in the Case Study movement the same excitement in the exposure of "materials, expression of structure, and the diminished separation of indoors and outdoors," but constantly showed how to "stretch [that] line further."[11] In contrast to the first Case Studies, the Mauer House takes a much more adventurous and comprehensive approach to the logic of the open plan; to the elimination of boundaries between terrace and house, vista and enclosure; and to the economy of freeing space to achieve that. By essentially building a miniature aircraft hangar, an "independent roof structure on plywood bents," Lautner left the house "susceptible to any kind of division of space" while the "informal handling of glass allows views and light, but is still human by being articulated and broken up." The Mauer House immediately took its place in architectural magazines as a model for what California could teach designers about the already burgeoning postwar suburb. Even more striking, though it came more slowly, was the response in the national popular press. *Ladies' Home Journal* used the Mauer House in 1949 to place Lautner with Carl Maston and Richard Neutra as the leaders in a movement that had made Los Angeles the incubator of ideas for new patterns in American middle-class living. *Holiday* magazine—in a New Year 1950 issue looking forward to a new decade in which America would adopt the Los Angeles model of free space, mobility, and open living—chose the Mauer House as the single work of architecture to make this point. It was the open-plan, indoor-outdoor house of the future—the pioneer in a California movement whose echoes could already be heard around the world.

Mauer House, Los Angeles, California, 1946:
view of interior

## JOHN LAUTNER, ARCHITECT

On June 12, 1947, Lautner wired his mother to tell her he was "separated from Douglas . . . on my own with plenty of work already . . . more ideas, brighter future, opening instead of closing." Having fallen in love with his partner's wife, Elizabeth, Lautner severed ties with both Honnold and Marybud, and took over the Honnold house at El Cerrito Place, with its studio garage and draftsman's apartment. He moved in his assistants Jim Charlton, Emil Becsky, and Jim Langenheim, to start his own practice. Elizabeth's daughter, also named Elizabeth, remained with them in the Honnold home, and after four years and a second marriage Marybud went home to Michigan. By now, Lautner recalled in interviews, he had "pondered for years . . . observing nature and different kinds of spaces" and "had a backlog in my mind of things I wanted to do."

Almost as soon as his independent practice opened, that backlog of ideas poured out into what became the most productive two years of his entire career. Lautner later marveled at his own productivity when, comparatively unhampered by lenders and regulators: "I could keep fifteen jobs in my head—every single detail. . . . I could get a house in complete working drawings in two or three weeks." The practice flourished because of the accelerating demand for rapidly constructed homes in a city that was filling up with returning veterans and their families. For twenty-six consecutive months after the war, Los Angeles County had more housing starts than anywhere else in the U.S. By 1947, with an average of nearly two cars for every three inhabitants, the city was voraciously converting a complicated patchwork of open land—bean fields, oilfields, hillsides, desert, and ranches—into a network of highways, subcenters, roadside services, and single-family home suburbs. The city's horizontal, centerless pattern of extension, based on a culture of motion that had governed it for thirty years, now began to look like a probable postwar future. For a short time, every step taken to design for this revolutionary new fabric, Lautner's included, was watched around the world. In the next forty years—the life of Lautner's practice in the region—this picture would shift, contract, and expand many times. But the exchange, improvement, and development of real property and its infrastructure would remain the primary employer and the leading creator of wealth in the region. In this changing rhythm of eternal city-building lay the source of Lautner's work, of the vagaries in his practice, of his reason for staying, and—in the growing resistance of its developers and lenders to take risks—of the conditions that led to his frustration.

Lautner's independent career is therefore marked by a pattern of booms and busts, the work changing course markedly after each hiatus. His essential works were made in four short, decisive but widely separated periods. From 1947 to 1950, as work tumbled into his office and out of his head, Lautner tackled almost every one of the new building

*above* Moreno Highlands, Silver Lake district of Los
Angeles, 1939
*right* The newly constructed Hollywood Freeway at
Cahuenga Pass, Los Angeles, 1950

types and conditions emerging in the experimental climate and economy of the mobile city: the "growable" house for the small family, the bachelor home, the sloping and hilltop house lot, the highway drive-in, the automobile showroom, the street-front highway workplace, the motel, the garden apartment court, and the community recreation center. By the spring of 1951, he was down to a single assistant, broke, and running up debt.

In a second burst of activity, starting with the research on Silvertop in 1956 and continuing through 1963, he would introduce radical ideas for the convenience store, the shopping center, the new town, and the open school, and, at the famous Chemosphere, the standardized house of the future. Beginning with the wood and glass of the Pearlman Mountain Cabin (1957) and accelerating as he began to uncover the poetry of poured concrete, he now focused on the tension between quietude and vitality and on the dialogue with light and landscape, making every work in any setting a kind of retreat.

Lautner launched a third phase of intensely inventive work from 1968 to 1973 with the shifting geometries of the modest suburban Walstrom House (1969), which is fitted to an impossibly steep lot, and a compact town house rendered in twin catenary curves for the Stevens family (1968), on an impossibly tight one. These years were most clearly marked by a revolutionary fluidity in planning and shaping space for the large houses that dominated his practice in this era—from the radical but still geometric lines of the Elrod House (1968) in Palm Springs to the absolute irregularity of Mar Brisas (1973) in Acapulco. These masterworks began to speak to the ethereal and transitory qualities of their settings, in what Lautner referred to as patterns of "disappearing space."

A modest revival in his practice after 1979 is marked by a shift into a sort of architectural geology—elastic spaces that draw on cave or shell forms but are punctuated by moments of almost crystallographic sharpness. It begins with the Segel House (1979) for the Malibu shore and effectively ends with designs conceived in 1983. These oceanside or mountain villas vary in scale, but all—as shown in the beautifully conceived Turner House (1982) in Aspen—establish a transcendental dialogue between distances and shelter, the solid and the insubstantial. These last two periods of astonishing virtuosity and invention pushed against so many barriers that they were checkered by compromise or outright cancellation, sometimes leaving only a suggestion of the governing idea on the ground or the most persuasive ideas entirely on the drawing board.

The breaks in Lautner's productivity had many causes. The Korean War slowed all construction from the fall of 1950 to the end of 1953. The lack of an architect's license—which Lautner did not gain until the late 1950s—shut him out of the Cold War boom in public building. In 1960, a catastrophic fire struck his house on El Cerrito. It burned to the ground, along with many of his drawings and papers, and drastically interrupted his work. In the mid-1970s, construction slowed down massively, in the aftermath of the oil crisis of 1973. Lautner became increasingly dependent on the "three or four people per year who wanted real architecture"—and they wanted homes that were increasingly dramatic, luxurious, and publishable. He was, therefore, collecting minimal fees to develop well-researched, site-generated, structurally innovative projects for private houses, each one contingent on the continued good fortune and goodwill of single clients, on the consent of regulatory agencies, and on the willingness of contractors to work in new ways.

Lautner's was a singularly uncertain practice, peculiarly sensitive to publicity and fashion. From 1947 to 1952, his work was met with respectful, sustained, and widespread interest. But toward the end of this period—as part of a growing movement to mock the culture of Southern California—the architectural press began to look askance at his contributions. Offended, Lautner largely—and disastrously—avoided architectural journals for the rest of his career. At the same time, he became famous for all the wrong reasons. The popular media sensationalized Lautner for over twenty years. It started in the early 1960s with reports on the extravagant "nightmare" of Silvertop and the worldwide portrayal of Chemosphere as an exercise in excessive futurism; it continued through the 1970s with a satirical *Playboy* account of the building of a pool for one of its editors, with Hollywood's repeated use of his houses to represent dystopic glamour, and with a burst of notoriety over the sheer scale of the Hope House (1979).[1,2] Each of these assaults coincided with major exhibitions of his work—in 1950, 1963, and 1973–1975—and thus undermined any serious reassessment of his contributions. Only in the last decade, when the drawing board was nearly empty, did a modest series of exhibitions and interviews, a film documentary, and the final appearance of a monograph begin to redress this imbalance.

This was a solo, even solitary, design practice with all the virtues and idiosyncrasies that came with it: a profound knowledge of process, structure, and materials, since he had to work them out himself; an assiduous concern for clients, with whom he worked so directly and intensively; and a deep, unmediated individualism, tailor-made to particular client needs and psychologies and intensely reflective of a personal ideology and of the shifting meditations and moods of his life.

From 1956 to the end of her life in 1979, Elizabeth—a Christian Scientist—was horribly afflicted by disease, and for the last two of those years Lautner was devoted, with her nurse Francisca (who became his third wife shortly after), to caring for her. One reflection of that long tragedy may be found in Lautner's spaces that speak to permanence and to its contradiction, the dissolution of fixed horizons. He grew to want a corporeal architecture that stayed fixed and incorruptible, and an ethereal space within it that absorbed the changeability of the elements around it. In the same way, the growing effort to bring the building into a transcendental discussion with its setting echoes his growing reliance on wilderness as a restorative force. During difficult times, he retreated to Midgaard and to his land at Three Rivers in the Sierra Nevada, land that he had bought to remind himself of the Lake Superior woods. His chronicles portray Los Angeles as a kind of gaudy and frenetic prison: "Back to Junkland," he wrote on May 28, 1990, "to fast food, fast deals, fast everything." His stepdaughter poignantly recalls his life in Southern California as a state of endless exile from the landscapes of his childhood and from the lost but "ideal world" of the Taliesin of the 1930s.[3]

Although this nostalgia for nature set his imaginative boundaries in architecture, it should not shroud the essential up-to-dateness and gaiety with which Lautner packed his life. He devoured the monthly news and popular science magazines, filing away endless clipped glimpses of a possible social and technological future. He loved the jazz clubs of Central Avenue, and musical, drinking, and talking parties; and he seems to have lived in a cabinet of joyful miracles. "The culture he made for himself," remembers his stepdaughter Elizabeth Honnold, "was startling. . . . The El Cerrito house, which was a big white-shingled, pitch-roofed California bungalow, was crammed with stuff he loved to look at—play with—stir around. . . . After the fire in 1960, he and my mother moved up the street to a large apartment with an outdoor eating balcony off the kitchen. More stuff was acquired—including a life-size papier-mâché Japanese tiger that stood on the grand piano, various Far East toys and games, bright wall-hangings, his mother's watercolors in plain white mats, full bookshelves, a fine stereo system and upgraded records of everything from Jellyroll Morton to Walter Gieseking's Schumann and Wanda Landowska's Bach. It was truly a wizard's cave of both large and small artifacts from around the world and down the street. He had rocks and stones of intriguing shapes, he had manzanita branches and ceramic geisha pillows, he had paper lanterns and teetering piles and piles of architectural publications." Taking the place of pride were "photographs of the Lake Superior woods and shoreline. . . . [for] John never left the Upper Peninsula [of Michigan]— it was his Rosebud, his Holy Grail, his lost heart's home."[4]

### A Landscape of Ideas

Throughout this essay, except where quoted as published, Lautner's statements on projects are taken primarily from his typescript project descriptions and notes, of which there are numerous sets compiled at different times between the first short statements for press and exhibition in 1947–50 and the compilation of the Artemis monograph in 1991–94, sometimes commingled and brought forward. Less frequently I have drawn on notes in client files, and from notes, drafts, or transcripts of interviews and biographical statements, 1971–94, identifying these documents specifically wherever distinguishable. These materials, primarily in the John Lautner Foundation (JLF) but with some strays and additions in Lautner Family Archives (LFA), await sorting and classification at the time of writing. The primary books thus published on Lautner are Barbara Campbell-Lange, *John Lautner* (New York: Taschen, 1999); Alan Hess and Alan Weintraub, *The Architecture of John Lautner* (New York: Rizzoli, 2003); and Frank Escher, ed., *John Lautner: Architect* (London and Zurich: Artemis, 1994).

[1] "His imagination was never corrupted by the limitations usually imposed on humans during the process of growing up within a social setting. He maintained an almost virginal attitude . . . ," Kamal Amin in Frank Escher, ed., "Lautner: A Tribute," *Journal of the Taliesin Fellows 18* (Summer 1995): 5-44, p. 20 [hereafter cited as Escher, "Lautner: Tribute"].

[2] Arthur D. Dean to John E. Lautner Sr., 29 January 1917, Lautner Family Archives, Deertrack, Michigan [hereafter cited as LFA].

[3] "Together we bring up the youth in this place—the older two by words and deeds; I by silent example. I will let the soft air of summer sweep across the rooms of childhood. . . . I will hold up my straight lines that he may see the straight way. I will show him my simplicity that he may learn sincerity. I will lay before him my simple decorative effects that he may feel the importance of a touch of the esthetic on a background of solidarity. I will stand firm on my foundations that he may know the value of integrity. I will line my walls with books that he may know of the world of thought. . . . I live for those two who built me. I live for the child whom together we are shaping into high ideals. . . ." Arthur D. Dean, *The House Speaks*, privately printed, August 1913, LFA.

[4] See Nathaniel Hawthorne, *The Scarlet Letter: A Romance* (Boston: Ticknor and Fields, 1850).

[5] Vida Cathleen Lautner, "Midgaard—A Family Project," *Progressive Education 4*, no. 4 (October–December 1927): 313–15. p. 315.

For the senior Lautner's background and ideas, see his manuscript course and curriculum chronicles while a student in Germany, c. 1899–1901, LFA, his "American Materialism" and other published essays, obituaries, announcements, and clippings in Lautner Papers, Marquette County Historical Society, Longyear Library, Marquette, Michigan, which also hold biographical notes and clippings related to Vida Cathleen Lautner. Vida's ideas and thinking are well represented in letters to Frank Lloyd Wright and the Taliesin Fellowship in the correspondence files of the Frank Lloyd Wright Foundation Archives [hereafter cited as FLW].

For the Marquette city home, see also Joy Wheeler Dow, "'Keepsake'. . .", *American Architect* 118, 28 May 1918: 702–4; "Seventeenth Century Salem House," *Daily Mining Journal* (Marquette, Michigan), 8 August 1939.

For Midgaard, see also Vida Cathleen Lautner, "'Midgaard': A Norse Cabin on Lake Superior," *Home Building*, June 1927: 12–13; *Daily Mining Journal* (Marquette, Michigan), 31 January 1927; B. L. York, *A History of Middle Island Point*, privately published (Marquette, Michigan), 1943: 62.

Lautner's own recollections of his philosophical grounding and summaries of his ideas are best recorded in his interviews, notably the unpublished transcript of a long discussion with Henry Whiting, June 1988 [hereafter cited as Whiting, 1988] in John Lautner Foundation Archives [hereafter cited as JLF]; in the transcripts of his interviews with the UCLA Oral History Program, 1982; in the prologue, epilogue and interview of Frank Escher, ed., *John Lautner* (London: Artemis, 1994), and in manuscript notes for biographical entries, notably that c. 1990 from which the Midgaard quote is taken (LFA).

### Ideas into Architecture, 1933–1938

[1] "At Taliesin, May 13, 1934," in Randolph C. Henning, ed., *"At Taliesin": Newspaper Columns by Frank Lloyd Wright and the Taliesin Fellowship, 1934–37* (Carbondale and Edwardsville: Southern Illinois University Press, 1992): 43-44 [hereafter cited as Henning, "At Taliesin"].

[2] "At Taliesin, August 23, 1934," in Henning, "At Taliesin," 71–72. I have attributed the quote on page 72 to Lautner, based on his notes and letters at the time.

This account of Lautner's introduction to and career in the Taliesin Fellowship is based on correspondence (FLW, JLF, LFA) between Lautner and Wright; on letters between Vida Lautner and Abby Beecher Roberts and both Wright and the Taliesin Fellowship; and among Lautner, his parents, fellow apprentices, and his wife (LFA).

See also Whiting, 1988; Lautner's unpublished interviews and biographical notes in both LFA and JLF, notably Jo Walker, "Lessons from Practice: An Interview with John Lautner," *Architecture California* 13, no. 3 (1991): 42–47 [hereafter cited as Walker, *Architecture California*]; an unpublished video interview at Taliesin, 19 February 1989 (FLW) [hereafter cited as Taliesin, 1989]; a letter to Olgivanna Wright, June 1981 (JLF); and from published memoirs of Taliesin Fellows, especially Cornelia Brierly.

Lautner's readings and writings from his student years through his Taliesin apprenticeship—including his marked copy of the endsheets from Wright's *Modern Architecture* (Princeton: Princeton University Press, 1931)—appear in notes in LFA; full drafts of writings and Taliesin talks, including Lautner's discussion of the Broadacre small house and the Roberts House, are found both in LFA and FLW. Many were adapted for contemporaneous publication in Wisconsin newspapers and in the Taliesin newsletters, and a number are collected—often as revised by Wright—in Randolph C. Henning, ed., *"At Taliesin": Newspaper Columns by Frank Lloyd Wright and the Taliesin Fellowship, 1934–37* (Carbondale and Edwardsville: Southern Illinois University Press, 1992).

Wright's ideas have been drawn from published and unpublished letters and talks to students at this time and from the Taliesin Manifesto of December 1933 (FLW); and from Bruce Brooks Pfeiffer, ed., *Frank Lloyd Wright: Letters to Apprentices* (Fresno: California State University Press, 1982): 93.

For the notes on Wingspread, which Lautner assisted Wright in compiling, see the special issue of *Architectural Forum* 68 (January 1938): 56.

### The Small House Problem in America

[1] Frank Lloyd Wright, "The Small House Problem in America," TS in *At Taliesin* files, n.d. [March 1934] (FLW).

[2] Edgar A. Tafel, "The Small House in Broadacre City," TS as above, n.d.

[3] Frank Lloyd Wright to John Lautner, n.d. [September] 1938, LFA.

[4] Frank Lloyd Wright to John Lautner, n.d. [February] 1939, LFA.

[5] Frank Lloyd Wright to John Lautner, n.d. [November] 1939, LFA.

[6] George and Velma Sturges, interview transcript, 29 April 1992, Taliesin Oral History, with (FLW). (hereafter cited as Sturges 1992).

[7] "A Hillside Redwood House designed by John Lautner," *California Arts and Architecture* 57 (June 1940): 27.

[8] Sturges 1992.

[9] "House Against the Horizon," *California Arts and Architecture* 59 (June 1942): 23–25, 23.

[10] *California Designs* 1, no. 1 (August 1947): 511. Raymond Kappe in Escher, "Lautner: Tribute," 24.

[11] Raymond Kappe in Escher, "Lautner: Tribute," 24.

     Lautner's work with Wright in these years has been reconstructed from correspondence between them (FLW, JLF, and LFA); Lautner's letters to his mother (JLF and LFA) and correspondence (JLF and LFA) with Taliesin Fellows and former Fellows, including Henry Klumb and Jim Charlton.

     Letters between Lautner and Whitney Smith and Samuel Reisbord (LFA), along with pay stubs and other documents allow some for reconstruction of his wartime career.

     Memoirs and interviews quoted and used for this period include Lautner's radio interview with Nancy Pearlman, 1989; Whiting, 1988; Taliesin, 1989; and the biographical statement made for the San Diego AIA chapter in 1977 (all JLF).

     Descriptions of built work by Lautner in this period are taken primarily from project notes and summaries in his office records (JLF)—some prepared at a later date—and from statements prepared for publication at the time. For publications of the built work of this period in addition to the citation in notes above, see "New Angles on a Slope," *House Beautiful* 83 (June 1941): 66-67 and *House Beautiful Building Manual* 13 (Fall–Winter 1941): 40–41 [Lautner residence]; *The Californian*, December 1948: 48–49 [Bell], *California Designs* 1, no. 1 (August 1947): 16 [Bell and Mauer]; *Ladies' Home Journal* 66 (November 1949) [Mauer]; Hamilton Basso, " Los Angeles" in *Holiday* (January 1950): 26–48, 31 [Mauer].

**John Lautner, Architect**

[1] John Reese, "Dream House or Nightmare?" *Saturday Evening Post*, 20 August 1960: 30, 62–64. [hereafter cited as Reese, "Dream House . . ."]

[2] Bernard Wolfe, "Swimming in Red Ink," *Playboy* 11 (July 1964): 93, 98. [hereafter cited as Wolfe, *Playboy* 1964]

[3] Elizabeth Honnold, letter to Nicholas Olsberg, 20 June 2006.

[4] Ibid.

     This section is drawn primarily from correspondence and interviews between the author and Lautner's family, friends, and associates, especially his daughters Karol and Judith, and his stepdaughter Elizabeth; from the memoirs published in Escher, "Lautner: Tribute"; and from oral history and interview materials notably those in the University of California, Los Angeles, Whiting 1988, and an interview in *Opus Incertum* (Journal of the University of Texas School of Architecture), April 1985: 10–11 [hereafter cited as *Opus Incertum* 1985] and published in Walker, *Architecture California*. Manuscript visitors' books known as the "Three Rivers" and "Midgaard 'Chronicles'" in the LFA shed great light on Lautner's private moods and reflections toward the end of his life.

Lautner in his office, c. 1957. The exhibition panels behind him illustrate the exterior and interior concepts for Henry's Restaurant in Pomona and a view of the interior of the Gantvoort House.

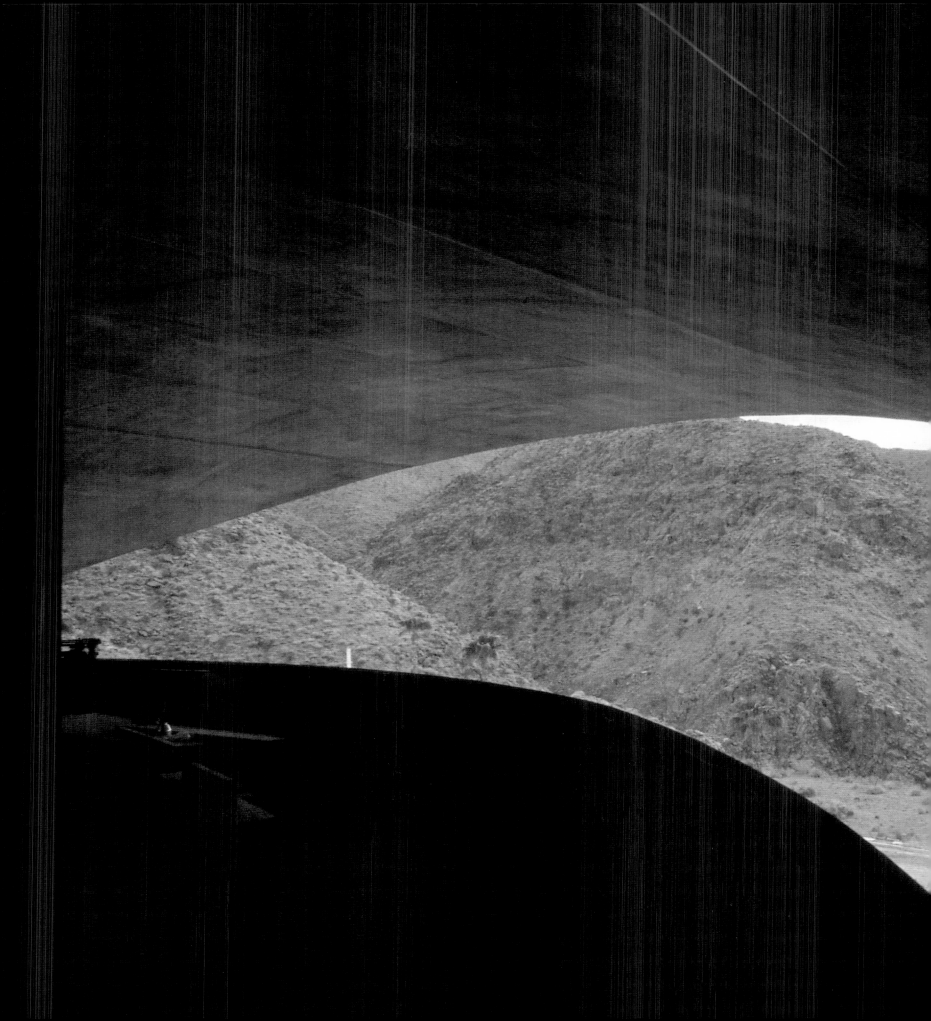

# 3

BUILDING

# SHAPING AWARENESS

Nicholas Olsberg

## NEW PATTERNS FOR LIVING

Architecture, Lautner said shortly after opening his own practice in 1947, was simple—"as little a thing as enclosing a space, whether for work or living, that has the right feel for the human being on *his* part of *his* world . . . working in 'living' conditions and living in 'working' conditions."[1] This early theoretical statement held three principles that would govern Lautner's work in the next years: that "all the functions of life are spatial experiences"; that architects should design toward proprietorship, so that the temporary denizens of desks in an office or booths in a diner or dwellings in a crowded urban landscape should have the sense of owning the space they occupy and the vistas it unfolds; and that cityscapes should be made of consonant rather than disparate forms. An architectural language, Lautner suggests, should not make distinctions between private and public, or work and living spaces: industrial materials could support a house or fashion a car showroom; the determination to free space from the tyranny of the bearing wall and to loosen the movement between indoors and outdoors could apply as equally to a market as to a garden apartment or a motel suite; and the movement of sunlight over sheet glass or the view of the horizon could be as carefully framed in a roadside diner as in a family kitchen.

This approach to new patterns of living commenced with a series of small houses for hillsides that floated their roof structures above an undivided space. "The idea began," Lautner noted, "with an attempt to provide flexibility—to erect an ample roof and floor, which could be closed in serviceable areas. These areas are conceived to be completely fluid, either permanent or to be rearranged for future use. The non-structural walls can serve as anything from screen cabinets to curtains. As much or as little of the building may be enclosed as desired, making easy 'inside-outside' arrangement for any orientation."[2] The first of these experiments, for the Polin (1947) and Jacobsen (1947) houses, were twinned on adjacent sloping sites to demonstrate their adaptability and repeatability. "The hexagonal steel roof is designed to fit any lot, level or hillside . . . supported at three points which dig into the ground for firm support without cumbersome retaining walls," Lautner wrote about both houses.[3] "There are the three supports

*page 70* Hope House, Palm Springs, California, 1979
*below* Polin House, Los Angeles, California, 1947: sketch, exterior perspective

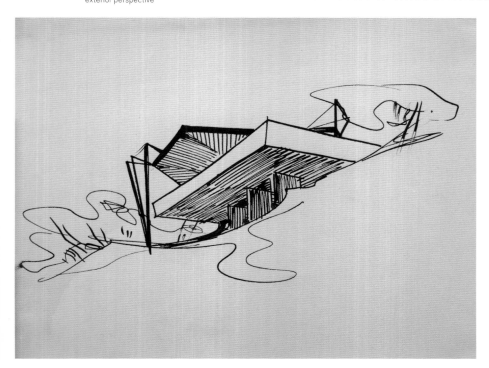

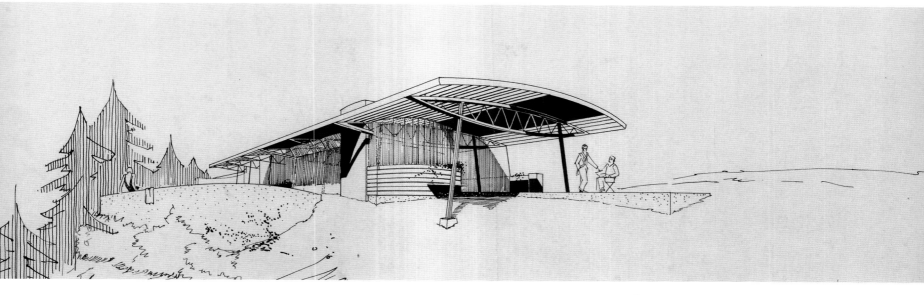

Gantvoort House, Flintridge, California, 1947: presentation drawing, exterior perspective

and by a lengthening or shortening one or two . . . it fits any kind of a hillside," he said later. "And then by making them good for taking the horizontal forces as well as vertical forces, you can have glass all the way around . . . without any sheer walls."

For the independent, floating roof on a flat site, Lautner took a different approach. In the Gantvoort House (1947), for a retired Dutchman from Java with a collection of dark and densely etched, crosshatch-detailed Indonesian furniture, he sought to bathe the collection in light and echo its details in the structure, and he designed a simple independent steel truss roof on splayed pylons—a fixed pavilion with no supporting walls. "Erected first as for a factory," and in two days, it "not only allows open plan, clear glass, etc.—but owner-builder can finish without getting lost."[4] These "elastic living arrangements," became even more pliable in the Carling House (1947). Using the same three-point suspension posts as the Polin and Jacobsen houses, the Carling House allowed an entire wall to roll out to form a windbreak on the terrace; this made it "an amphitheater in summer and a solar house in winter." Lautner was especially concerned with giving Carling, a bachelor who worked from home, the sense of a sheltered but changing place, "private, permanent—yet *free*."[5] In this, his most ambitious, tailored, specific, and expensive house to date, Lautner began with an intense study of the site—drawing geometries up from the ground and vistas through the house out beyond it—and of his client's "personality, physical needs, professional needs, [and] avocation."

The three-point structures of the Polin, Jacobsen, and Carling houses would not adapt to a major shift in scale or to projects on more than one level. For this, Lautner looked to Wright's Jester house project (1938) and to its arrangement of pavilions in the form of cylindrical drums. He tried this first in an unrealized project for the Abbots, a four-unit, repeatable apartment complex in which the cylinders were simply stacked into two storeys. He slowly realized a more liberal exercise for a sloping lot in Westwood Village for the artist Helen Sheats (herself the designer of a modular steel home in Madison, Wisconsin, before the war) and her husband Paul. Here, eight small rental units were to be topped with a penthouse apartment for the Sheats. This, a once common Los Angeles typology peculiar to the region until its postwar boom, made the most economic use of a deep house lot and reconciled the tension between privacy and community. These U-shaped

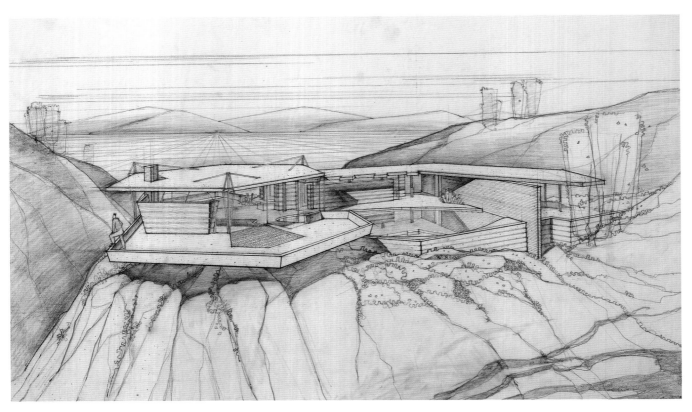

bungalow courts, with raised units at the top of the arc for the owners, could as easily march up a hill as along a level lot, and could bring everybody, from studio transients to retirees, into the same cloistered "colony." This typology always posed three problems, however, especially on a slope: parking, the dead space in the middle, and how to give every unit a view. Neutra's solution had been to eliminate the courtyard and set units back along terraced horizontal lines. But this removed the sense of community, made the transitional walking paths tight, gave better views to the higher units, and forced the dwelling spaces into rectangular boxes.

Helen Sheats desired something different. For each unit, Lautner recalled, the client wanted "a short walk and a long view."[6] Lautner gradually reached an extraordinarily generous and inventive solution. He separated the individual units, shaped each into a drum form, and set them on different levels with different orientations. By using parking to raise the complex above street level, Lautner opened the views to all and, in doing so, resolved the traditional courtyard apartment problems. "Eight apartments, about nine hundred square feet each . . . private terraces. No common walls—apartments seem like separate houses; full perimeter has light and air, privacy, balconies, separate entrances . . . from easy winding ramps. Interiors without bearing walls."[7] Sheats called it "a village of units," pinpointing what engaged Lautner so intensely in the design: it was the first realization of his democratic creed.[8] Each unit gave its occupant a unique space, an individual view, a private conversation with nature and the horizon, yet a unity with the whole through a common architectural language, materials, and a landscape of pathways, watercourses, and vegetation—including a gigantic tree rising from the center. Called L'Horizon (1948), it was a perfect expression of Lautner's purpose: "to keep the infinite variety of individual life within some kind of total world."[9]

In December 1948, the Sheats Apartments was still only half finished and virtually no new work was coming in. But he had three highly inventive small bachelor houses in advanced design stage—for clients Foster, Bergren, and Tyler, all in Los Angeles. National

defense restrictions on construction came
into force in 1951, and the last two of
these houses were not completed for some
years. All three drew upon the experiment
with compacted space of the L'Horizon units, carefully constructing in dense suburban
settings private worlds with an awareness of nature. The Bergren House (1953), looking
away from the city on the steep north slope of the Hollywood Hills, was built around a
single large living space that widened and shifted height as it floated out to an open terrace.
Lautner noted it as becoming a capacious shelter within a tiny volume by simply being "a
free floor set in a free space . . . so that when living there, one feels in the mountains and
out of town." The Tyler House (1953) gained its sense of space by being "a house with no
walls," and by how Lautner composed the access and outlooks to frame and claim a much
larger territory than the one it owned. The house for Louise Foster (1950) achieved the
same end by eschewing all retaining walls, setting up the roof on wood and concrete columns, siting itself to focus on "a private view" and blindsiding its curved walls to the street
to intensify that view.

About the same time, Lautner undertook the design of a much grander, hilltop
house for Leo M. Harvey. The site allowed a more expansive vista, but Lautner oriented
everything toward a single controlled exposure as he had with the three smaller houses.

*left* Carling House, Los Angeles, California, 1947:
presentation drawing, exterior perspective
*above* Abbot apartments project, Los Angeles, California,
1948: presentation drawing, exterior perspective
*below* "L'Horizon" Apartments, Los Angeles, California,
1948–49: sketch, exterior, drawing by John Lautner

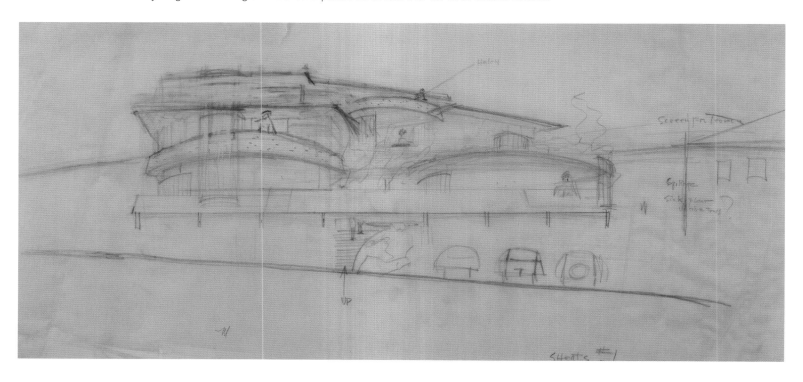

United Productions Animation Studios, Burbank,
California, 1949: presentation drawing, perspective

"The circle seems to me the best kind of plan for houses on hillsides," he said. "It gives you
the most panoramic view and follows the contours of the hill most easily."[10] He also saw
it as increasing the freedom of movement from indoors to outdoors. To make for Harvey "a
house that floats on a hilltop," Lautner changed the scale of the drum from the L'Horizon
scheme, using it to anchor four interlocking pavilions, and he carried the logic of the curve
in the circle into the outlying wings, out to the terrace and on to the perimeters of the
site.[11] Suggesting a windmill or propeller settling lightly onto the hilltop, it recalled Wright's
spiral crown for the hilltop in his 1924 project for the Strong Planetarium and the great
cart-wheeling plan of Wingspread. As the sense of flow and continuity at L'Horizon and
Harvey show, such radical geometries and structures derive not from any formalist or organic
theory of spheres and cylinders (such as that propounded by Le Corbusier and Amédée
Ozenfant in the 1920s) but from the search for shapes that will fit to each site a new freedom of space, movement, and vista—establishing in each setting a private imaginative
world of its own.

## SOCIAL SPACE IN THE MOBILE CITY

From the start, Lautner considered his highway constructions as well-flagged social spaces, not as conveniences carrying signs. We have probably forgotten the circumstances of such buildings: they had to be seen in time for motorists to leave the roadway; they had to be cheaply and quickly built with a lightweight structure; they had to guide traffic smoothly in and out; and they had to deal with the heat buildup from glass and the fumes of the highway. Lautner's most inventive solutions reside in two automobile showrooms of the late 1940s; a series of combination drive-ins and restaurants for Henry's; a roadside office building and animation studios for United Productions of America (UPA); and a neighborhood market for Beachwood Canyon. These works stress visibility, transparency, and openness, and stand as cool oases beside hot, fretful, dusty highways.

The showroom for Lincoln Zephyr (1948) in Glendale was fashioned with a tower visible to drivers approaching from a distance and with a display for those passing. Lautner's "open and patio-like" showroom was originally designed with a radiant floor to heat it in the winter; the dramatically rising, overhung canopy cooling it in the hot Glendale summer. Lautner carefully sketched the path of the sun, so that he could shape the canopy to display the merchandise without frying the salespeople. The showroom functioned at

*above* Lincoln Zephyr Showroom, Glendale, California, 1948: presentation drawing, perspective
*below* Lincoln Zephyr Showroom, Glendale, California, 1948: shadow and light studies, exterior perspectives

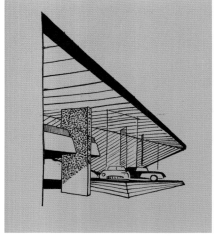

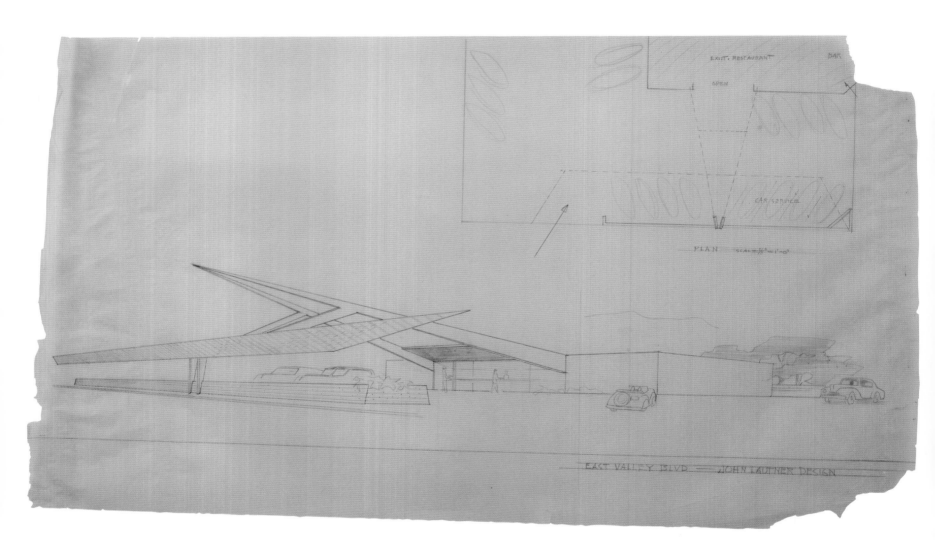

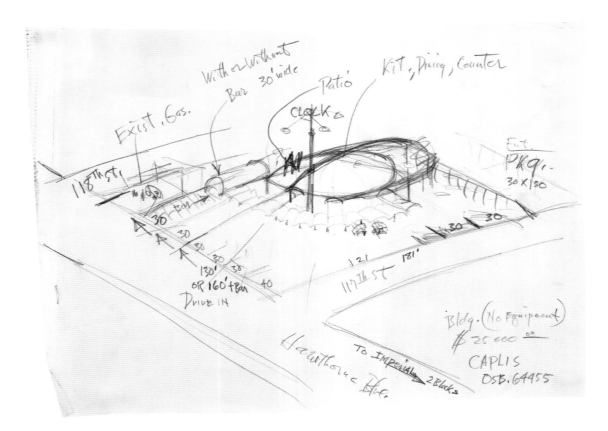

once as domestic courtyard and as a sort of starting gate, a place where visitors might imagine cars leaping from their blocks and onto the roadway. His early drive-ins, like the unbuilt project for Caplis (1952), had the same sense: they rendered the social space as light, isolated from traffic, and comfortable, while still landmarking entrances to flag the hungry driver. UPA Studios (1949) in Burbank, built on a forbiddingly low budget, was simply a long, open pavilion of artists' studios where everyone had "light, air, and a view." Lautner cleverly used color to signal its presence, enliven its workspaces, and animate the roadscape.

His determination to bring space, light, and vista to the simplest commercial conveniences gradually turned Lautner's roadside work into some of the most daring and generous experiments in architectural form. For Henry's Restaurant in Pomona in 1957, Lautner chose to shelter "all restaurant facilities [indoor and outdoor] under a single shell." He used prefabricated glue-laminated beams as a construction system and shaped them into a flying dome with a single spine. The roof and its overhang gave a view to all, made the indoor and outdoor spaces invitingly sheltered yet open, and—though set back to accommodate parking—used the rising shape of the building itself as its roadside landmark. In remodeling the small Beachwood Market (1954) in Los Angeles, he lifted and lit the cavernous space first by changing the street front into a cambered, skylit glass wall, rearranging the goods into concentric circles, and allowing the interior to rise up to its street wall in an extraordinary inverted catenary

*left* Henry's Restaurant, Alhambra, California, 1959
*above* Caplis Drive-In restaurant project, Hawthorne, California, 1952: sketch, exterior perspective

left and below Henry's Restaurant, Pomona, California, 1957
right Henry's Restaurant, Pomona, California, 1957:
study, site plan

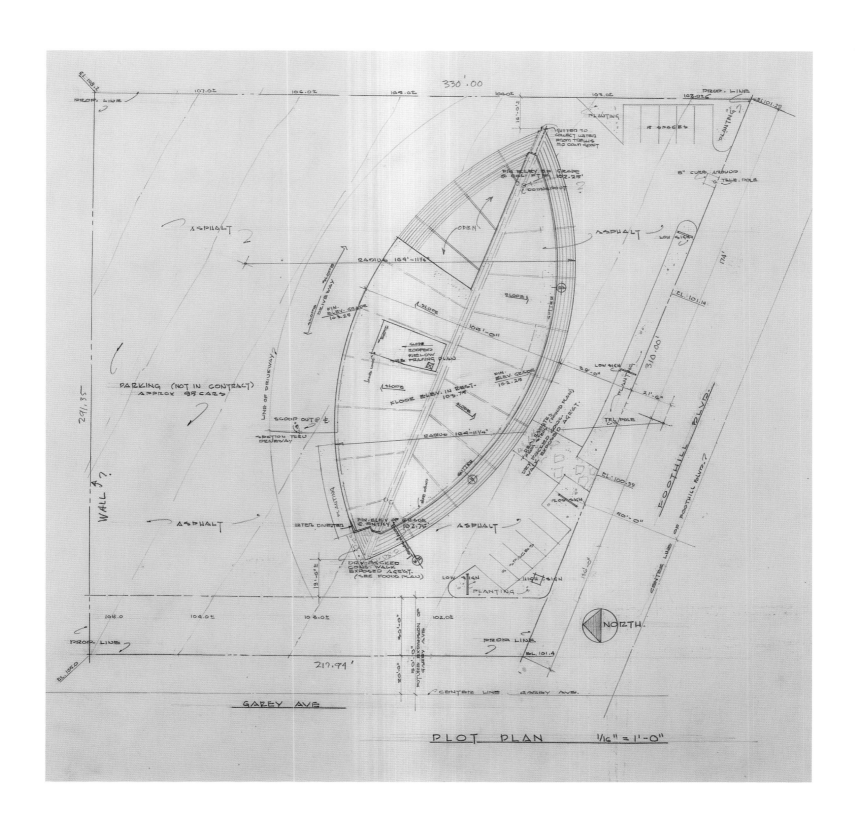

PLOT PLAN    1/16" = 1'-0"

*above* Beachwood Market remodeling, Los Angeles,
California, 1954: study, exterior perspective
*right* Googie's Coffee House, Los Angeles, California, 1949

curve. This ski-jump of laminated wood filtered light deep into the market and drove the eye upwards to the sky. The curved lines of solids and merchandise played off the angled planes of tilted glass wall and soffit. At both Henry's and the Beachwood Market, Lautner's distaste for the "dead" light and shape of a flat ceiling led him into topological territory that, with the fluency of concrete as inspiration, he would explore intensely in much of the work that followed.

Lautner's most famous highway work was a flagship Googie's Coffee House (1949), built entirely in steel at a time when shortages were making wood and concrete difficult materials for structures that had to go up fast and cheaply. Steel, however, was being produced under price controls at wartime volume, it was readily available from the local aeronautical industry, and it caught the eye in streetlight or sunlight. Googie's was startling not only for its gleaming mono-material of sheet metal and steel posts, but for a radical shaping of space: Lautner reversed the standard plan of a diner with its counter and window benches turned to the kitchen, so that guests now looked out to the view and away from the service areas. As at Beachwood, he avoided the common roadside strategies of landmarking the building with a signed front facade, or using a plate-glass front to reveal to the passing driver an eye-catching colored screen inside—making the sign an integral part of the form, uniting walls, tower, and roof into a single exposed steel-frame structure. Experiments with sheet metal and steel frames quickly ended, however, as supply became strained by the demands of re-armament, industry, and the 1952 steel strike.

By 1952 Lautner's work had been widely published. The Carling residence led off a *New York Times Magazine* issue on hillside homes, and his first three houses repeatedly appeared in popular and shelter magazines. But an assault now began, and it came on four fronts: against the inclusion of roadside commercial architecture into the architectural discourse, as *Architectural Record* had systematically been doing with drive-ins and motels, showing Lautner's work to particular advantage; against urban dispersal; against California, the Case Study Program, and the aesthetics of *Arts and Architecture*; and against Lautner himself, as the embodiment of these tendencies. He was especially criticized for allegedly borrowing the trivial language of the drive-in and applying it to private space—the Foster House (1950) was held up as the most egregious example. "Are residential streets of the future," asked *House and Home*, "to be as exuberant as today's highways, lined with the fantasies of gas stations and roadside nightclubs?"[1] The assault crushed Lautner and colored the reception of his work for a generation. Worse, driven by these attacks, he adopted the posture of an eternally aggrieved outsider whose work would never be understood, and expressed his contempt for the architectural media—at the expense of being better understood—by avoiding them.

### SENSING THE TERRAIN

"When standing on a site, he seeks its particular and unique expression with all his senses," Lautner said of himself in notes for a biographical statement, "equally exploring his clients' desires and moods—until the natural setting, the character of the owners, and the design harmoniously become a single idea." On a windswept sun-baked shelf facing Mt. San Jacinto, Lautner came to the first of the expansive landscapes from which his most radical work would take flight. The Bubbling Wells Resort (1947) at Desert Hot Springs was part of a thirty-acre development

Bubbling Wells Resort project, Desert Hot Springs, California, 1947: printed promotional perspective

project—it was to have ninety six-hundred-square foot homes, an outdoor spa, and a connected line of one-room dwellings for visitors organized as an infinitely extendable motel. Only the spa and four visitors' units were ever built. The spa was conceived as a set of wide-angled glass windscreens, overhangs, and water terraces set above the desert floor, echoing in horizontal planes the 45- and 60-degree lines of the topography that rose around the site. The motel repeated the angled geom-etries at a smaller scale but reversed the siting strategy, digging into the ground to frame the sky at shoulder height, turning the living space away from the horizon toward a narrow sheltered garden, and screening the patio, which projected out onto the desert floor, with "sky-lit" walls. Public space was thus tailored to the desert's shifting vistas, and private space to the settled picture of its nearer earth and its sheltering sky. The two approaches to the Desert Hot Springs scheme—one sheltering to "draw in" the sublime, and the other

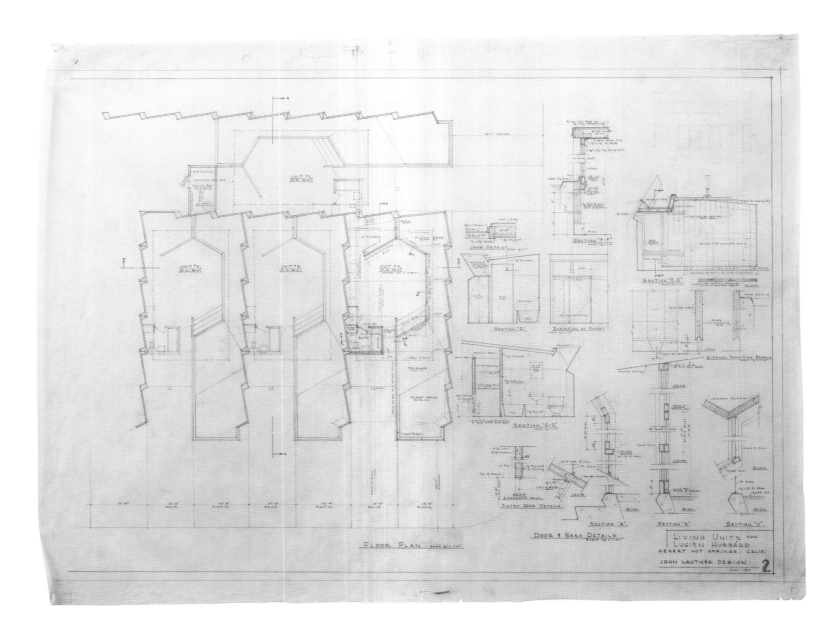

*above* Desert Hot Springs Motel, Desert Hot Springs,
California, 1947: construction drawing, ground-floor plan
*left* Desert Hot Springs Motel, Desert Hot Springs,
California, 1947

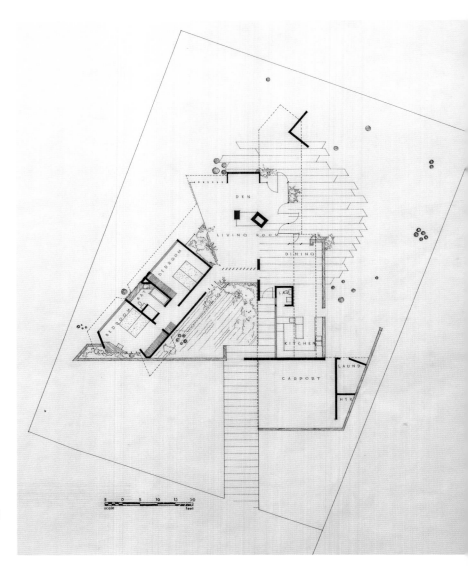

opening to "radiate" toward it; one reflecting its geometries and scale, the other contracting them into a counterpoint—would form the core of Lautner's discussion with the wilderness for the next forty years.

Two other projects of the late 1940s brought Lautner's structures into nature: the Eisele Guesthouse (1947) in the Hollywood Hills and the Schaffer House (1949), designed for the parents of an assistant, in the quiet valley setting of Montrose. The Schaffer House was Lautner's first residential project without a horizon, a distant vista, or the sense of a dissolving sky. Instead, he dwelt on the

rhythms of light in the grove of live oaks, building between the trees in two vertical layers, one of redwood boards and the other of mullioned glass panes, to create the sense of an unbroken transparent screen. The wandering plan, as Lautner described it, was "designed to fit in between trees and see trees from inside," the wooden boards and roof talking to the trunks and canopy of the oaks, and the walls dancing to the shards of sunlight that fell between them. An early scheme for the Eisele Guesthouse high above Los Angeles was Lautner's first exploration of concrete structures. He shaped it as a single inverted section of a catenary curve. At the same moment as Le Corbusier experimented with ways to vary his concrete *voiles* between the pierced and the solid to make abstract patterns of light and matter, Lautner left some blocks void and glazed, but his was a more musical rhythm, closer to Piet Mondrian. The result would have been penetrated with light and opened to a sheltered vista: absolute enclosure in absolute brightness.

Both projects took their cues from the ground, but neither distilled the geometry of site in quite the same way as the series of houses that began in the 1950s with the Shusett residence. The Carling and Harvey houses found their forms in a rhythm of natural geometries. At the Harvey and Schaffer houses, he spread the ground plan and separated living zones into interlocking volumes with independent scales and articulations of the governing geometry. With the Shusett House (1950), he extended both ideas. He took the large pine tree at the center of the site as his pivot point, spun a dispersed plan around it, and used a tree trunk and its manufactured cousin, the wooden dowel, to organize both the circular system governing the general plan and, at differing scales, the structural system—down to the ordinary wood rounds of its mullions and details. As at the Harvey House, and as he would do later at Silvertop, the Sheats, and the Elrod houses, Lautner united diverse elements of the site geometry into a set of individually shaped spaces that flowed together internally and fitted within the larger geometry of the plan, creating a coherent whole.

In the houses that followed, Lautner played with a multiplicity of topographic and organic geometries: space sculpted by interlocking circles; a cartwheel roof; a plan organized on a gridded suburban lot into a gridded trellis; and—finding teardrops in the undulation of a site—a plan of parabolas colliding at different scales. All were contrived, from the character of the site, to encourage the freest flow of spaces. The tension between the conditions of the site and the requirements of the client might have triggered these ideas: at the Hatherall House (1958), where privacy was paramount, the shapes emerged from the need to "[turn] its back on the street and let the open end face the view"; at the Concannon House (1960) the challenge was to bring in daylight from two sides of every room; and at the Tolstoy House (1961), on a spacious exurban site, an industrial solution using natural geometry—a set of petal-shaped polyurethane roofs, hung from cables—answered the client's request for a house that stretched out into the landscape with the most open living space possible. Even bolder was his design for the Owens Valley Radio Observatory (1968), where he chose a form evoking a compass. There was a studied integrity to these projects, each, in "the seclusion of its own landscape," organized around a recognizable geometric language of its own, and set in a single key to a steady rhythm, so that "the idea of the whole" is as much felt as seen.

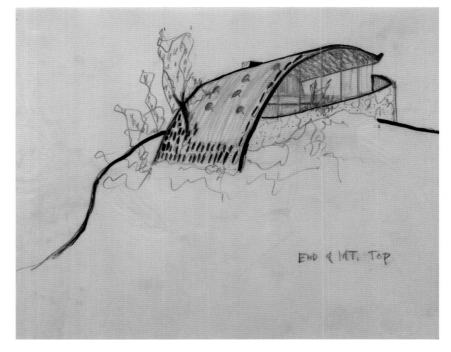

Eisele Guesthouse, Los Angeles, California, 1947: sketch, exterior perspective of preliminary scheme

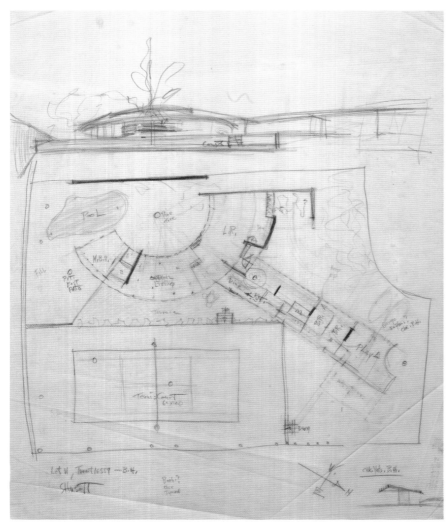

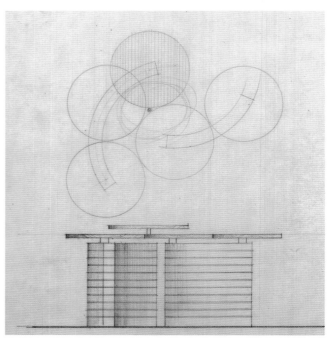

*top left*  Pearlman house project, Santa Ana, California, 1958: presentation model

*top right*  Shusett House, Los Angeles, California, 1950: sketch, exterior perspective

*left*  Shusett House, Los Angeles, California, 1950: sketch, exterior elevation and ground-floor plan

*above*  Shusett House, Los Angeles, California, 1950: study, plan and elevation of the patio furniture element

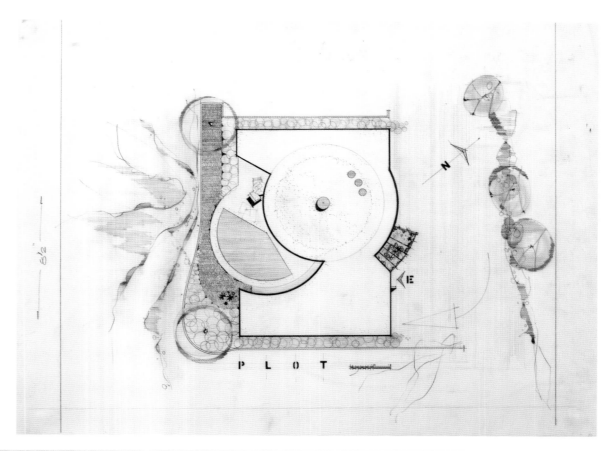

*right* Hatherall House, Sun Valley, California, 1958:
presentation drawing, site plan
*below* Hatherall House, Sun Valley, California, 1958:
presentation drawing, interior perspective

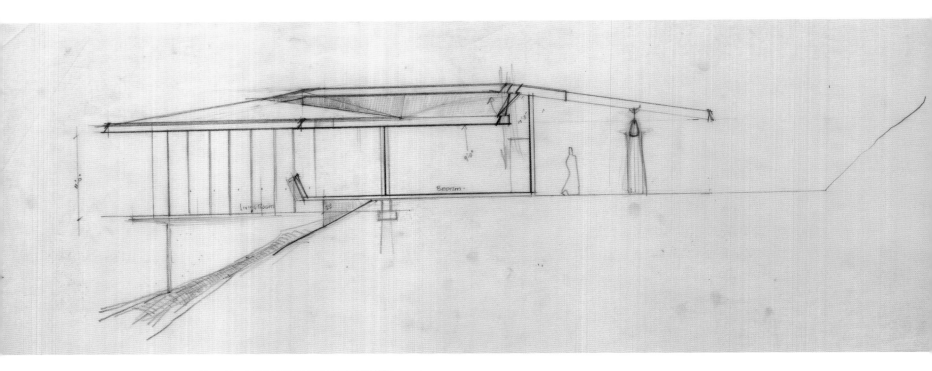

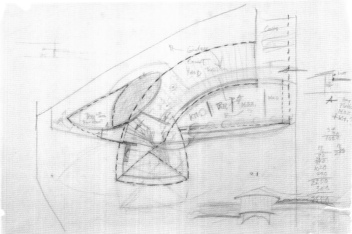

*top* Concannon House, Los Angeles, California, 1960:
study, cross-section
*above* Concannon House, Los Angeles, California, 1960:
sketch, site plan and perspective elevation
*right* Tolstoy House, Alta Loma, California, 1961:
presentation drawing, ground-floor plan

The Pearlman Mountain Cabin, whose design began in 1956, united these natural geometries with the wilderness setting of an intractably steep wooded slope in the Idyllwild arts community. For the course of an entire day, Lautner sat on the giant rock that rendered the site "unbuildable"—and then imagined an open cylinder with a platform deck around it, a circular roof hovering over it, and tree trunks supporting it. A serrated glass screen created the illusion of nothing between the shelter, the forest into which it was settled, and the skies and mountainsides beyond. Lautner talked of "the ceiling disappearing into the sky where the glass is opening to the woods." Light bathed this one-room house, moving like sunshine traversing a clearing. In this cabin, a sense of the terrain was always present in the play between open and closed, solids and voids, circle and angles, manmade structure and natural engineering. In a single compact volume, crystalline and circular geometries, and lustrous and rough surfaces mixed. Lautner wove together what orthodox architects would regard as irreconcilable: competing scales, conflicting materials, and disparate geometries. At the Pearlman cabin, the conjunction is absolute and abrupt—two different feelings simply welded together as independent segments of the same cylinder. The result was not a willed tension but a strange sense of repose.

Pearlman Mountain Cabin, Idyllwild, California, 1957

## CONCRETE AND THE CONTINUOUS LINE

As the Pearlman cabin design was emerging, a request came from the inventor and independent manufacturer Kenneth Reiner to develop a research house for his family that would test new materials and techniques for the market. With this project, Lautner began a six-year inquiry into construction systems and aesthetics. Reiner wanted to "point the way to new horizons in modern residential construction," to the problems that a 1960s family would want addressed, and to a "refreshing sculptural" aesthetic.[1] Put more grandly, it would be an essay in rethinking domestic space from top to bottom; and put more frankly, it would be one from which both parties might reap profit. The result was Silvertop, directly across Silver Lake from Richard Neutra's famous VDL Research House (1932).

With Silvertop, the scope of Lautner's work changed. In 1985, Esther McCoy called it the "progenitor" of the elastic forms and space from which the houses of his last twenty

years are made: "Walls disappeared. Roofs billowed and sailed."[2] Silvertop was a study in curves, but the key to the shift in Lautner's aesthetic ambition lay not in the discovery of the curve or even the parabolic, catenary, and elliptical, but in concrete as a material that, like a sail, could express a seamless flowing line.

Concrete, he said, was an "expressive form . . . like bittersweet, and other subtle things. . . . By the nature of it, it can take, become, continuous and disappearing spaces." At first glance, both the swooping form and the experience of its vast interior made Silvertop appear more like a public building than a dwelling. But Lautner's ambition to fold the changing horizon—time and vista—into it made it otherwise. As the light shifted and the water floated shards of sunshine up to the glass, it felt, as one of Lautner's clients said, like a pavilion in the sky—that space "between" that gets "near to heaven and wherever the gods may be."[3]

*above and left* Silvertop, Los Angeles, California, 1963: construction views, c. 1962

The popular press mocked this extravagant exercise: "Dream House or Nightmare?" asked the *Saturday Evening Post*, comparing Silvertop (1963) to a spaceship ready to "zoom off to Mars"[4]; and Reiner, nearing bankruptcy, sold it before completion. As Frank Escher discusses, for research on Silvertop, Lautner journeyed to Mexico and Europe to see thin-shell concrete structures, and embarked on an intensive study of structural engineering. But as his work moved into this free-form, abstract arena, he must also have been aware—if only from what was shown in *Arts and Architecture*—of the developing psychoanalytic and expressionist aesthetics of space and form: Ad Reinhardt's quizzical reflections on the emotional triggers of space; Sibyl Moholy-Nagy's analysis of the psychology of perspective; Garrett Eckbo's curvilinear reading of terrain; Alvar Aalto's and Paul Rudolph's use of bent plywood; Harry Bertoia's anageometries of form; Alessandro Nivola's fluid murals and sculptures; George Nakashima's rigorously a-geometric carved furniture.

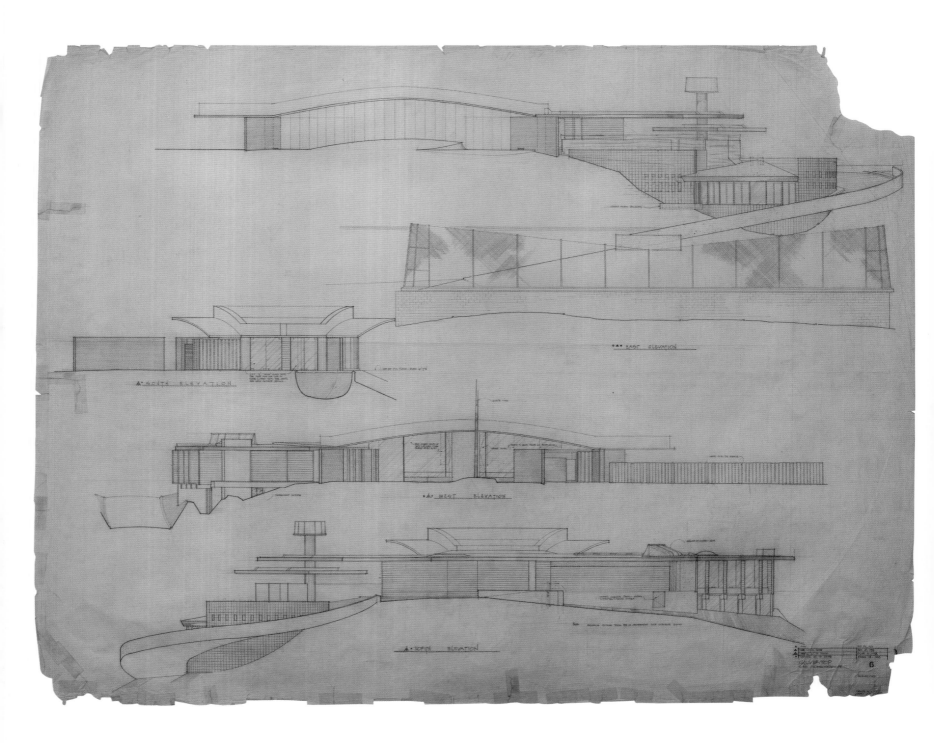

He admired Félix Candela, Henry Klumb, Oscar Niemeyer, Eero Saarinen, Hans Scharoun, Jørn Utzon, and Juan O'Gorman. Yet Lautner's work is looser and less mechanistic than most of these, and this quality derived from his methods and from his responsive, instinctual ways of thought. "The concepts all came out of his mind—to be sharpened and juggled on paper, perhaps, but already conceptually full . . . certain rather than fortuitous," recalled his daughter Judith, who worked with him for many years.[5] "When he picked up a pencil or folded a piece of cardboard," said Guy Zebert, who collaborated with him on structure, "you knew the job was done."[6] "I just put down the plan and section . . . the essence of everything," Lautner said, "And try to get someone else to draw it up." He added, "I don't believe in renderings . . . these double-curved things—they're almost impossible to draw," noting that he learned and said more with "a rough cardboard model, nothing fancy at all." He "thought more comfortably in three dimensions," concluded Judith Lautner, "Every part of his life . . . was ruled by his spatial reasoning, his sensitivity to light."[7] Structure, as engineer Andrew Nasser noted, was secondary: "Even though he designed with structural logic in mind, his priority was spatial freedom and sculptural excitement."[8] Lautner believed "that a building is a structural idea where structural components converge to articulate a space."[9] For someone who thought in terms of colliding structures and the space that could appear within them, the grid and the module were irrelevant. "I work almost entirely with curved things, and I don't seem to

*left* Silvertop, Los Angeles, California, 1963: construction drawing, exterior elevations
*below* Silvertop, Los Angeles, California, 1963: sketch, interior perspective

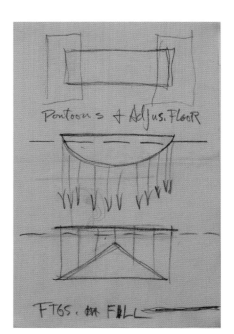

get any module out of them at all. In fact, what I strive for is the freest, most interesting kind of disappearing spaces and they are not susceptible to any kind of module."

### THE DEMOCRATIC VISTA

As postwar corporate America prospered and the Cold War space and arms races (based on the industries of the Los Angeles basin) accelerated, urban Southern California—still laid out in ribbons and patches—began to consolidate. While the city's sentimental memory of this era concentrates on demolished quarters like Bunker Hill and on the civic banalities that slowly took their place, the new towns growing up on reclaimed or open land better exemplify the era—Century City, Marina del Rey, or Westlake. Even grander projects developed at the same time: William Pereira's unbuilt schemes for the Ahmanson Ranch (1962) and Universal City (1961), designed with members of Archigram; Whitney Smith's California City (1957), a bedroom town set out in concentric circles; and plans for a corridor harbor town that would stretch from Newport to the new cities of Irvine and Costa Mesa. Some went up fast, some stalled, and others were built in fragments. It was an exhilarating moment in which the architecture and urbanism of the Modern movement worldwide took a visionary turn in real examples like Oscar Niemeyer and Lucio Costa's Brasilia (1959–70); in fanciful ones like R. Buckminster Fuller's Dome over Manhattan (1960), Kenzo Tange's Tokyo Bay (1960–61), or Yona Friedman's Ville Spatiale (1960); and in such new theories of urban space as "mat" or "field."

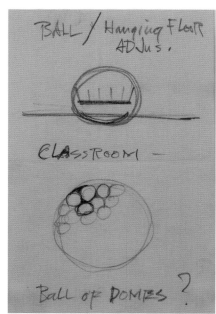

Lautner himself felt a burst of unaccustomed optimism in this space age environment, in which he saw a newly adventurous corporate world, a decisive movement toward a well-educated society, and a re-engagement of America with its expansive democratic spirit. In this mood Lautner made his final efforts to apply architecture to the reform of city and society, developing his dialogue with the environment and his structural experiments into highly original forms of planning and standardization. Turning back to his experience with Wright's Broadacre City, he began to speculate about a more open, democratic landscape and of the repeatable forms that might fit within. His thoughts took him beyond the conventional city, beyond the automobile, beyond the efficiently hygienic single-family house, beyond

*below and right* Midtown School, Los Angeles, California, 1960: sketches, plans, sections, and notes

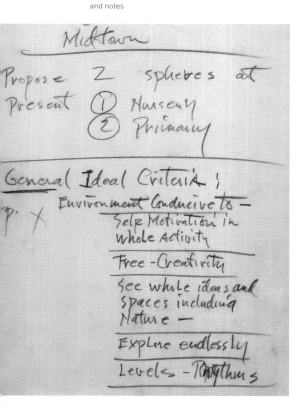

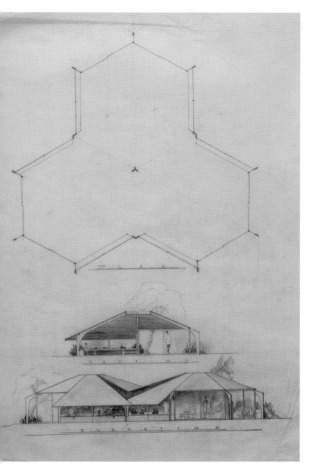

fixed patterns of schooling, and toward a broader sense of community, settled into extendable clusters with less-defined boundaries and a wider appreciation of space. Three critical projects mark this quest—a progressive school for the Reiners that could "expand to infinity"; the Chemosphere, a radical new model for urban housing; and a self-sufficient new town for Alto Capistrano set unobtrusively into the grassy canyons between the Pacific and the Coastal Range.

Lautner worked with the Reiners to develop the educational concept for the experimental early childhood Midtown School (1960). It was based on two pragmatic principles—the current explosive condition of education in Los Angeles, where in-migration and the baby boom were constantly stretching school facilities to their limits, and the need to protect children against a seismic upheaval; and on two theoretical ones—Lautner's longstanding belief that knowledge was born of "endlessly exploring," and his recent reading of Patrick Geddes and others on the relationship between learning and the psychology of space. Dealing with a fifty-foot-deep landfill, Lautner devised a system of repeatable lightweight forms on "floating slabs," their umbrella roofs resting on the thinnest curved space frames, and walls hung as mere screens. Like a tent stretched over a scaffold, each unit could stand on this urban "mat," either isolated or joined, offering both dramatic spaces inside and expansive invitations to approach the outside. Lautner's notes plainly show his intentions: a repeatable and infinitely extendable system that shifted scale from the infant to the infinite, opening the child to "seeing the whole" and the world beyond. It was quite self-consciously an educational campground in "midtown," designed to stretch out to its boundaries at will, and then perhaps to continue forever. The school quietly but forcefully inserted itself into a wider discourse: its forms are echoed in kindergartens

*left* Midtown School, Los Angeles, California, 1960: study, plan and elevation
*below* Midtown School, Los Angeles, California, 1960: presentation model, detail

throughout revolutionary Cuba, and similar approaches can be seen in the capsule systems of the Metabolists.

Chemosphere, Los Angeles, 1960: line engraving of a suite of imagined Chemospheres by Leavitt Dudley, published in the *Los Angeles Times*, March 11, 1962

For the Chemosphere (1960), Leonard Malin, a young aerospace engineer, approached Lautner with a minimal budget and an "impossible" piece of steep land on the south rim of the San Fernando Valley, but Lautner had enough time and imagination to invest in a workable model for a middle-class family dwelling. Lautner freed the Malin house from the hillside and placed it on top of a pole. The "one-column support," he argued, was not intended to sensationalize, but merely to be "sensible." Lautner told the *New York Times* that it was a variable prototype for "moderate-priced housing."[1] In a drawing for the *L.A. Times*, he showed a set of Chemospheres rising over the Hollywood Hills, and in one of his studies for housing at the hillside sites of Alto Capistrano, he briefly adopted the one-column principle for almost the entire new town before turning to a hexagonal unit system closer in feeling to that of the Midtown School.

For years, Lautner had viewed technology and materials from the aerospace industry as a way to put designs for housing into mass production, "the way Henry Ford did . . . [with] all the materials. All the machinery. And I would just manufacture it and say, 'there it is,' . . . things that could have quite a bit of variety and still have some repetition."[2] Although using aerospace materials and techniques at the Chemosphere, Lautner departed from the mechanistic and siteless visions of Disneyland's Monsanto House (1957) or Alison Smithson's House of the Future (1956), setting up a genial, well-lit family space within and a sympathetic relationship to the natural environment without—"penthouse living . . . without destroying the landscape." The local utility company and the manufacturer of the sealants and bonders used in the construction, both of whom sponsored its construction, promoted it as the "house of 1975," and the press—worldwide—followed their lead, mostly with scorn. London's *Daily Telegraph* featured it on the front page as a "flying saucer . . . the latest architectural fashion in California," and *Playboy* drew a prose portrait of Lautner "engaged in a struggle to the death with the force of gravity," dreaming of "airborne anti-G[ravity] peppermint-stick cities."[3] As late as 1984, critics still read the Chemosphere as "science fiction . . . combining technology with a

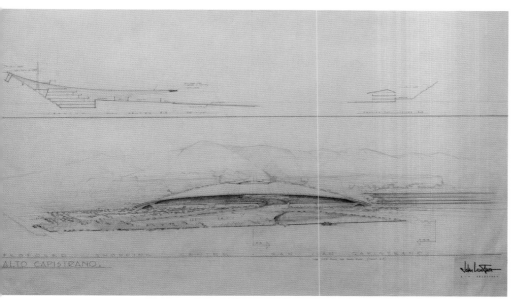

notion as old as history—the myth of the tree house, the retreat of modern man tyrannized by modern life."[4]

At Alto Capistrano (1963–69), Lautner developed ideas first seen in the L'Horizon Apartments and at the Chemosphere into "a total plan for living in ocean air and view, with maximum privacy and convenience, and with buildings in a form to suit the hills." He recognized only two viable ways to make a dense residential community: either layer smaller structures vertically, using different levels to maintain views and concentrating dwelling space to increase open space; or lay out much larger buildings into a low-lying mat, curving with the terrain to set up secluded landscapes. At Alto Capistrano he fused the two. The first and most exciting plan, for a population of ten thousand, was fully designed by June 1963, but the county was simply unwilling to accept the density Lautner had proposed to retain the landscape. The final scheme ended in 1968, when—with earth moved, roads being laid, and a hexagonal sales office in place to demonstrate the architectural language of the residences—the developer backed out, and the project was abandoned. The original plans embraced light industry and included a research park at the entrance; a park of "drive-in offices" in a wilderness landscape; two-thousand terraced apartments in concrete; double-storey town houses stacked and staggered into the slope;

*above* Alto Capistrano development project, San Juan Capistrano, California, 1963–69: study, perspective of main shopping center, c. 1963

*below* Alto Capistrano development project, San Juan Capistrano, California, 1963–69: study, general perspective of scheme showing shopping centers, hilltop apartments, and town houses, c. 1963

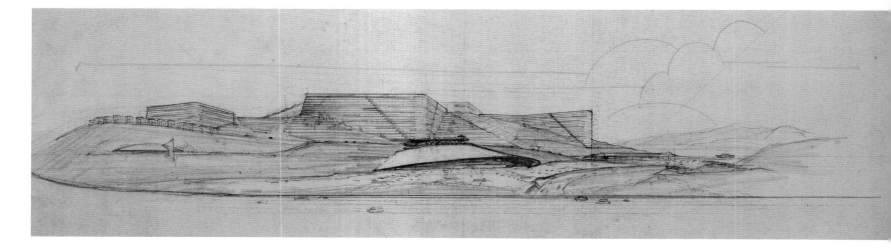

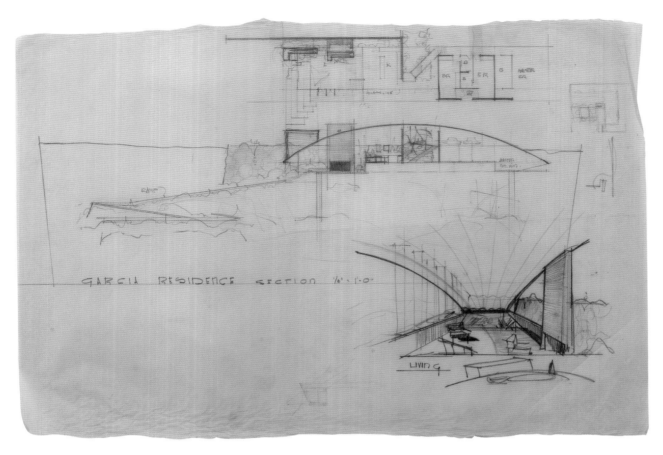

Garcia House, Los Angeles, California,
1962: studies, plan, section, and interior
perspective

convenience stores built into the dwelling complexes; a five-acre shopping center under
a single roof "suspended from the hillside"; and "planned parks . . . open spaces . . . pools,
and lakes throughout."[5] Of the eleven thousand acres in the scheme, only a few hundred
were to be disturbed. Most dwellings were tightly clustered and connected by "hill-eleva-
tors," with communal parking below and recreational facilities above. The living units fanned
out like fingers to obtain autonomous views and outdoor spaces. It was as if Lautner had
taken the logic of a high-rise and flattened it on to the hillside. Protecting the landscape,
building a sense of privacy within community, providing the sort of density and convenience
that were essential to families in which both parents were employed, and largely circum-
venting the need for the automobile, these were prescient experiments in designing a new
world for an expanding postindustrial society.

### SYMPATHETIC AND DISAPPEARING SPACE

Lautner followed Silvertop with a series of residences in varied suburban sites. For each,
he found a specific structural logic and architectural grammar to maximize—
through vista, light, and the flow of space—the experience of its setting. Lautner described the Garcia House (1962) as "lamellated wood arches [designed] to blend in
the hills" by taking the same form as the curved "hump" in the terrain. The house echoed
a more complex topography by splitting itself into two at a slight fold in the land—decisively
dividing the house into the two distinct domestic zones the clients required—and then
bridging the gap.[1] For a house for Marco Wolff, the narrow lot had an acute street-to-street
slope in a densely developed section of the Hollywood Hills, and he requested "something solid, private, permanent," suggesting fieldstone walls and a copper roof. Uniting
stacking and structure, cantilever slab and masonry tower, Lautner created a multistorey

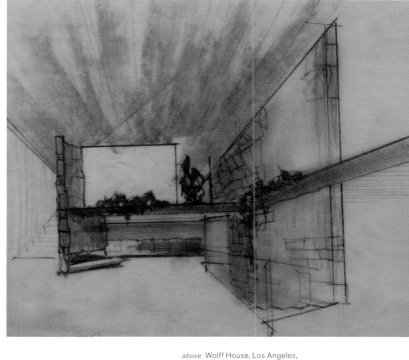

*above* Wolff House, Los Angeles, California, 1961: sketch, interior perspective
*left* Wolff House, Los Angeles, California, 1961: study, interior and exterior perspectives

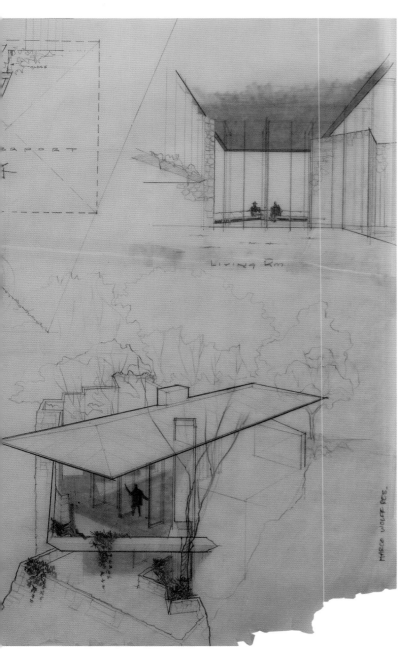

house with two habitable levels. It clung to its hill and turned against the incline to steal private outdoor space. Whereas Silvertop was essentially panoramic, the Wolff House (1961) was narrow, exploiting its tower form to deepen the perspective of the views and control the vista, thus liberating the prospect from its urban context.

In his Bel Air house for Helen Sheats on another steep site, Lautner cut a shelf into the hill and allowed the house to recline on it. "One day while I was at his studio," Sheats recalled, "John began folding paper and arranging it on the topographic model. Suddenly, he had three triangular folded plates hugging the hillside, and the basic scheme was formed."[2] Like the Garcia House, the Sheats House (1963) had a decisive split between its two main living zones: a linear suite of private spaces sat along the shelf, and the plan then turned through a dining hub to open onto a triangular projection with a dramatically angled roof, which covered the main living space and opened to the pool. The roof, at the intersection between sleeping and living zones, drooped like an elbow, and the cantilevered living pavilion ended in a beveled edge that suggested it might stretch to infinity. Lautner pierced the roof with drinking glasses, which, like the trees in a forest,

brought filtered light into the cavernous setback. The whole effect was like living in the folds of origami, with a carefully framed prospect that stretched forever.

Under the extraordinary patronage of a new owner, James Goldstein, Lautner revisited this project for "a modern villa" in his last years, scrupulously refining and polishing it to meet the terms of the times. The more modest and functionalist scheme for the Walstroms, in contrast, stands just as happily unchanged. At the Walstrom House (1969), on a steep slope on the north side of the Hollywood Hills, Lautner was faced with making a light-filled private world at a much more modest scale. With the rising and turning of its changing levels, the vast height, and subtly shifted geometries of the open living space, he achieved an extraordinary sense of space and of movement.

As Lautner intensified the dialogue between building and landscape, he focused increasingly on connections—the sense of continuity accomplished through extending into the natural site, establishing a rhythm consonant with that in the natural context, and drawing in both outside space and the phenomena of light and sky. He spoke of this both as a quest to crystallize the patterns of these elemental forces within the structure and as an essay in shaping the building to make it reach out or radiate toward these forces. Ever freer and more varied forms emerged from this dramatic conversation between the space within and the space without. The Harpel House (1966) in Anchorage, Alaska, on the shores of a suburban lake looking south, was designed to make the long dark winter livable. It revolved around a single idea: to draw in a palette of light, setting a curved, reflecting, yellow-gold wall deep into the house behind its window wall to pick up the horizontal winter sun and bring its glow right into the center of the house. At the Goldsmith House (1964), the requirements were visual. The client asked for "the color or atmosphere created in an abstract

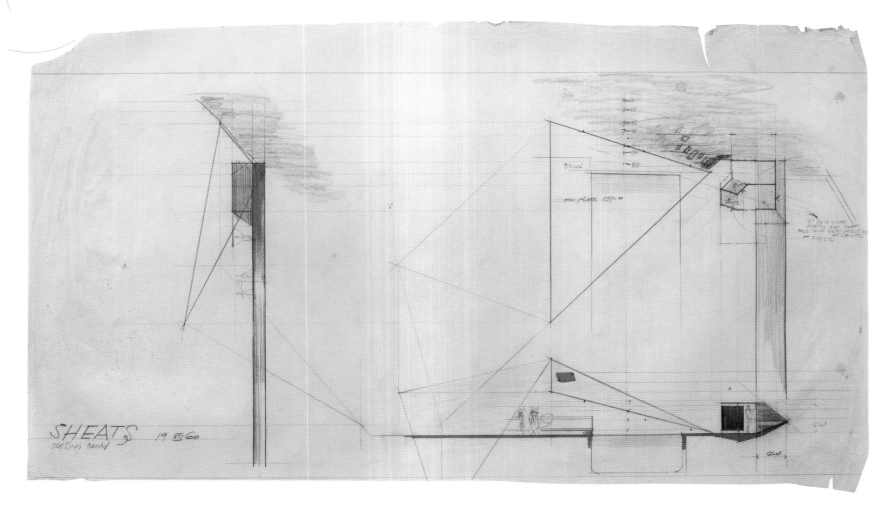

SHEATS 19 XII 60
DRESSING ROOM

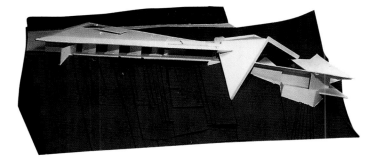

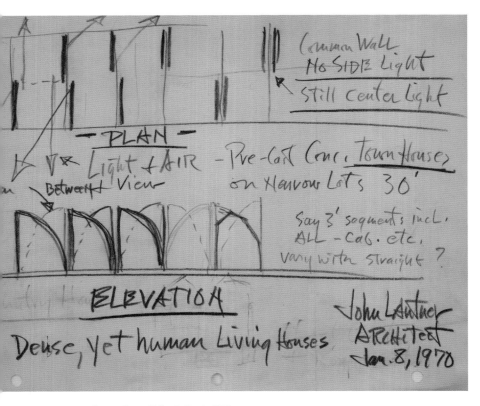

— PLAN —

Light + AIR

Between View

ELEVATION

Dense, yet human Living Houses

Common Wall
No SIDE Light
Still center Light

Pre-Cast Conc. Town Houses
on Narrow Lots 30'

Say 3' segments incl.
ALL - Cab. etc.
Vary with straight?

John Lautner
ARCHITECT
Jan. 8, 1970

Stevens House, Malibu, California, 1968:
sketch, section showing the concept for
concrete town houses

painting—so he got skylight, clerestory, reflecting walls, green views," a fusion of the palette of inside and outside into a single, discrete landscape and a consequent "integration of the senses."

The Stevens House (1968), perhaps, offered the most striking example of landscape drawn inward. Here, on the tightest of oceanfront sites, the client wanted a spacious five-bedroom house. Only two solutions seemed possible, Lautner told the client: the cave or the fishbowl. The fishbowl it was. The house was two, simple overlapping concrete, catenary curves that brought light, space, and the theater of the ocean into the deepest reaches of the narrow lot. Working on a ridge above Palm Springs on the interior designer Arthur Elrod's house (1968), Lautner asked, "What makes the whole space?" and he answered, "having the ceiling be a reflection of the roof." The combination of black floor and massive dome shielded the space from the fierce brilliance of the desert sun and heightened the brightness and color of the view beyond. Elrod—at once buried and protruding, cutting into the rocky ridge so that it draws the desert boulders into its form, and hitting the sheer edge of the slope so exactly that it seems to jut out over the valley below—almost magically manages to reconcile this extraordinary play between the psychology of being settled and the transcendence of moving into another world. By this stage, Lautner was describing himself as "part psychiatrist, part metaphysician."[3] Everything about Harpel, Goldsmith, Stevens, and Elrod speaks to that dialogue.

The Elrod House is perhaps the last example in the long line of distributed plans, starting from the Shusett House, in which Lautner radiated the zones of the building into distinctive segments that spread out from a central point, often to the perimeters of the site. With the Stevens House, and the Harpel House in Alaska, Lautner discovered that one could move in and out of a distant landscape more effectively by staying in the same spot, using the fishbowl effect of compacted space to enlarge what lay around and beyond it. As a result, Lautner's spaces became much more plastic and subtle, concentrating on fluent containers, but folding controlled elements of the outside world into them. For the Franklyn house project (1973)—designed to overlook

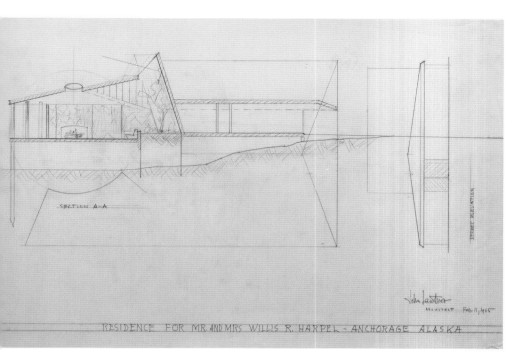

RESIDENCE FOR MR. AND MRS. WILLIS R. HARPEL - ANCHORAGE ALASKA

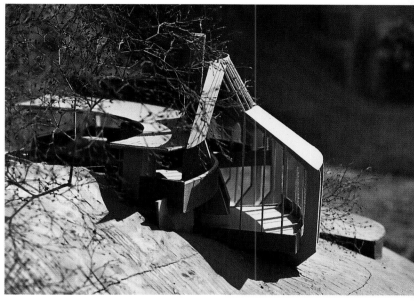

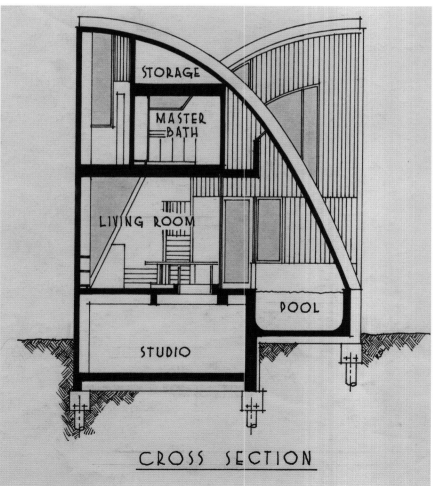

STORAGE

MASTER BATH

LIVING ROOM

POOL

STUDIO

## CROSS SECTION

*top left* Harpel House, Anchorage, Alaska, 1966: study, section
*above* Goldsmith House, Los Angeles, California, 1964:
study model
*left* Stevens House, Malibu, California, 1968: presentation
drawing, section

*far left* Elrod House, Palm Springs, California, 1968: view of interior through living room, as remodeled
*above* Elrod House, Palm Springs, California, 1968: view of the roof of the garage and bedroom wing
*left* Elrod House, Palm Springs, California, 1968: study model

a riding oval, a paddock, and a polo ground in the feature-less pampas of Argentina—Lautner first shaped the house into what resembled two segments of an ostrich egg, setting those sheltering ovoid curves up onto stilts. Like the stands at a racetrack, the whole dwelling thus observed its prospect. A second, equally adventurous, Franklyn scheme modified its shape and dropped it closer to the ground. For the cliffside beach house for the Familians (1976), five descending levels and a mix of curved and linear geometries shaped space and motion, and an open court drew in a landscape made up almost entirely of the sky above.

This idea of the building as an observatory that magnified its surroundings appeared again in an unbuilt project for a Nature Center in Griffith Park (1973). Lautner produced two divergent schemes: one in which the observatory was buried under a mound that opened up to reveal the world above, and the other in which it was placed under a "monolithic concrete roof structure to create an up-and-out space, incorporating trees and park beyond the building" so intensely in the view that they seemed to have entered the building. In both schemes he actually achieved the same effect: "the ceiling disappears into the sky and only nature is visible." In Palm Springs, for Bob and Dolores Hope (1979), he perched a vast birdlike form on the desert hillside and used a garden court and pool beneath it to draw the outside in under its wings.

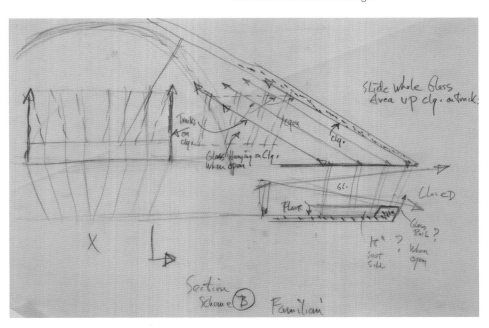

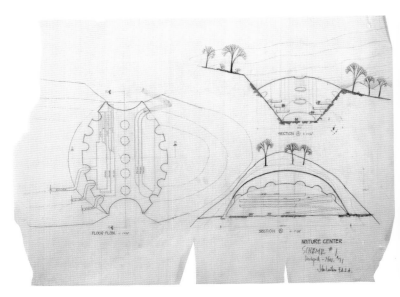

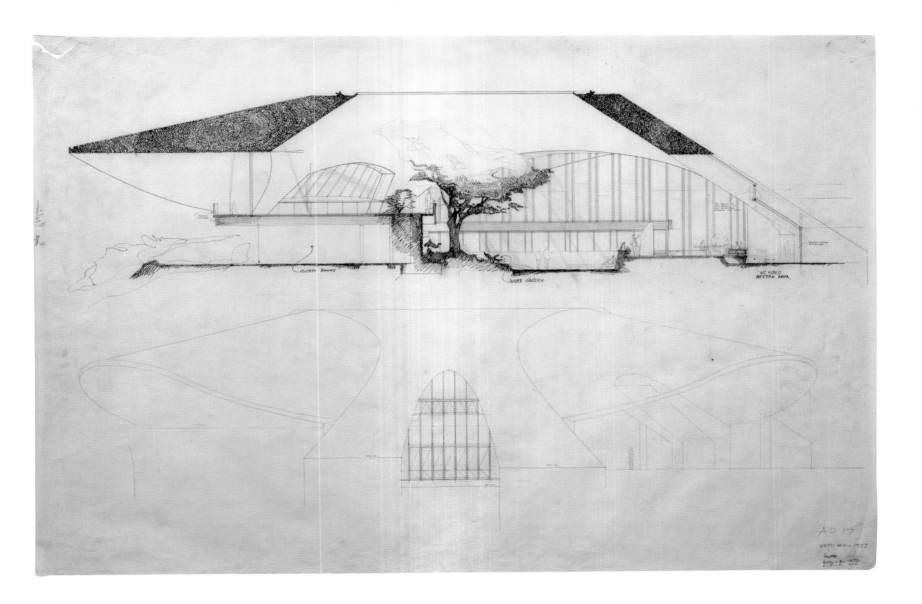

top left  Franklyn house project, Buenos Aires, Argentina,
1973: study model
far left  Familian beach house project, Malibu, California,
1976: study, longitudinal section
left  Griffith Park nature center project, Los Angeles,
California, 1973, sketch, plan, section, and elevation of
preliminary scheme
above  Hope House, Palm Springs, California, 1979:
study, section

Mar Brisas, Acapulco, Mexico, 1973: view from the living room

The Mar Brisas villa (1973) in Acapulco opened Lautner's eyes to an even wider view of the dwelling as observatory: the possibility of suggesting "disappearing space." Lautner asked the house to "transcend its own mass," drawing the senses to the evanescent light and indefinite geometries distant from its immediate setting. Hence its spaces, most of them open to the elements—although retaining their sense of being shaped by solid structure—twist, turn, and sometimes dissolve entirely to reflect the changeability of the horizon and the accessibility of the intangible. Taking this idea of dissolution to its extreme, Lautner began to reach for an economy of form, with which he could "dissolve the confines," thus removing all sense of mass and enclosure. In projects ranging from an office suite for his patron Jim Goldstein in a curtain-wall urban high-rise to an unbuilt retreat for himself at Three Rivers in the Sierra Nevada wilderness, nothing but reflectivity, color, planar geometry, vista, and light remained to create the transcendent illusion of being freed from the structure entirely and inhabiting the space beyond.

## THE EXTENSION OF THE SENSES

In 1973, as Mar Brisas villa was reaching completion, a major Lautner exhibition traveled across Europe. Uneasy over the purported exclusiveness of his work, the organizers suddenly adapted this retrospective and presented him alongside perfectly forgettable Los Angeles work, none of it bearing the slightest relationship to Lautner's ideas. As a result, the critical essays in the catalogue focused on precisely what Lautner was not: avatar of the spirit of a casual, disorderly, sprawling, and unstructured city of gaudy neon and cheap symbolism. David Gebhard, echoing the received opinion of Silvertop ("a Flash Gordon city on the moon") and Chemosphere ("a flying saucer from outer space"), dismissed the work as outdated, merely a "union of current technology with nineteenth-century Romanticism." Reyner Banham, who had once admired the logic of the Chemosphere, now called him nothing but a fabricator of "one-off dream houses." Yona Friedman labeled him the last example of a noble but outmoded breed—"the architect as artist-psychoanalyst"—rather than an instrument of a changing society; and Hans Hollein, though he recognized and came increasingly to admire the emotional force of Lautner's plasticity, saw in his uninhibited individualism the anachronistic procedures of the nineteenth-century.[1]

In fact, recognition of the expressive force of Lautner's explorations of structure and plastic forms had been slowly growing. A wide-ranging exhibition at Art Center College of Design in Pasadena at the end of 1963 and a compendium of his work in *Arts and Architecture* in 1965 had already begun to dispel the sensationalism around his work. In 1971, *Architectural Record* named the Stevens House the House of the Year. Others were starting to acknowledge that Lautner had dramatically expanded the language of architecture with the fluid volumetric geometries that had once been confined to the shaping of a hull, a barrel, a vat, or a bunker. Structural engineer Edgardo Contini, in testimony to the AIA, countered the notion that his work translated space-age structures into architectural form, insisting that Lautner was "not borrowing forms suggested by engineering ingenuity, but coaxing the engineer into giving expressive form to structure."[2] Esther McCoy suggested this when she wrote for a 1985 exhibition: "The mind that conceived them is supple as a *spline*; the instrument that recorded them is a compass with an ever-changing radius."[3]

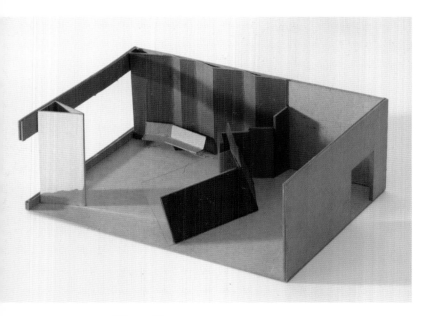

*above* Goldstein Offices, Los Angeles, California, 1989: study model
*right* Goldstein Offices, Los Angeles, California, 1989

Lautner, however, noted that McCoy missed the metaphysical idea this shaping was meant to evoke, not grasping that the suppleness of space extended to the folding of time, expressed in the contradictions "alive, free, but still at rest, solid." This is a complex idea, but it is what Raymond Kappe suggested when he referred to Lautner's curved forms in concrete as opening architecture to "a new dimension."[4] Indeed, the idea that a building can suggest temporal flux within its permanence, and stillness under its physical fluidity, now dominated Lautner's work. He called this "freedom," meaning not a looseness of form, but a formal originality that could liberate perception.

This notion places Lautner close to artists like Clyfford Still or Agnes Martin, Jackson Pollock or Barnett Newman, whose work he knew and followed. He also equated his architectural procedures with those of the composers he loved. He talked about the "open forms" of Duke Ellington; he knew the work of Miles Davis, Olivier Messiaen, Carl Ruggles, and Morton Feldman, in which a new structure emerges for every work; he spoke of music where the silent "spaces" between the notes became as important as the sounds, similar to how the voids and distances made his architecture; and he talked of jazz forms that the listener could not predict, but which, like the slowly unfolding unfamiliarity of his architectural spaces, seemed inevitable once uncovered. In the same way, we can see in Constantin Brancusi the idea that a freestanding work of art can create an aura around itself; in Donald Judd the illumination of surrounding space; in Mark Rothko an awareness of something being thrust forward from within; or, as Lautner himself said, in Willem de

EL. 2005

EL. 2025.5

STONE
SEAT.

BREAKFAST TABLE
4'-0"

EL. 2024

EL. 2032

EL. 2017

14 RISERS

14 RISERS

EL. 2030

20" OAK

LOUNGE

28" HIGH

COUCH

50'-0"

PAINTINGS

PAINTINGS

BOOKS

10'-0"

PINE

KITCH.

ENTRY

7'-0"

JOHN
WALK-IN CLOSET
6' x 8'-6"

17'-3"

10'-0"

28" HIGH

ELIZABETH
WALK-IN CLOSET
7'-6" x 8'-6"

BATH
TUB

16" HIGH

16" HIGH

PROPERTY LINE

NORTH

Kooning, the dissolution into nothing but light, reflection, and hue—a dispensing of "line and form to make shapes simply from color."

In notes for an interview, Lautner defined "reality" as "the intangible universe in relation to man." By now Lautner could say that the palette with which the architect must work was nothing but "light and air and sun and freedom and space"—so that revealing the ineffable became the primary task. The building, he argued, exists only as we perceive it, and this we do differently as light and memory play upon its surfaces and into its voids. Hence it moves, grows, changes, and becomes "alive." At the very least this suggests the need to avoid—as Lautner's work invariably tried to do—the fixed point of view or the single moment at which the whole of a structure and space can be embraced. To achieve this, space should be shaped to awaken the senses to what could not quite be seen—the rhythms of life, nature, and the universe.

Lautner's understandings of the 'real' went back to Goethe and Kant, and he often presented it as a synonym for 'beauty', suggesting that if an object has achieved a

*left* Lautner mountain cabin project, Three Rivers, California, 1974: study, plan detail
*below* John Lautner mountain cabin project, Three Rivers, California, 1974: section elevation

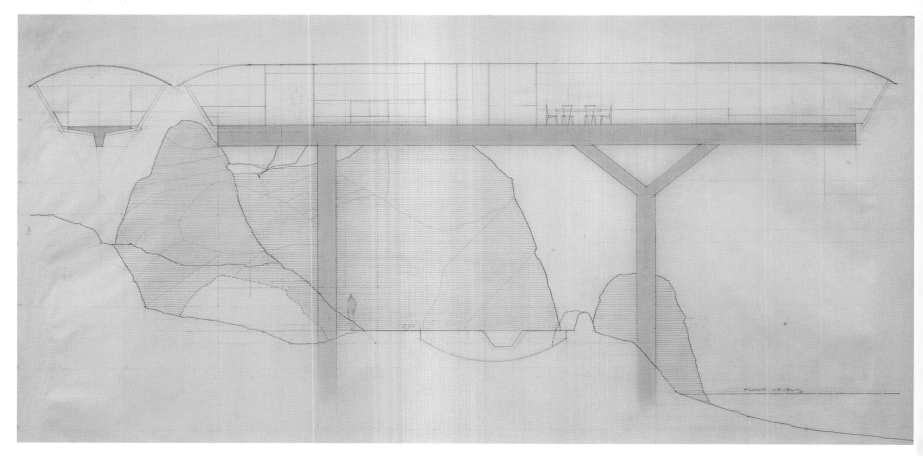

natural order of its own (the 'real'), it has a satisfying inevitability that can be sensed by all ('beauty'). In some places he called the sum of this equation "common sense," and in others "sincerity." "Integrity" was simply the means of carrying the equation out—ensuring a sympathy between form and function, structure and expression, or materials and shape, and between details and the sum of the project—the "integral" relationship between "openings, ornament, and the whole." The object of this search for beauty was "freedom" or "joy", terms in Lautner's vocabulary—as they were in Goethe's or Friedrich Schiller's or Ludwig van Beethoven's—that stood for two aspects of the same idea.

Lautner's late works use sensory depth to obtain a metaphysical power. Asked at the time to identify which moments in architectural history he admired, he replied that the only one that still interested him was the age of "basic caves, huts, etc." Only sheltered space, he believed, could liberate observation enough to "ignite the imagination and excite the spirit." Starting with the Segel House (1979), cave, shell, and waveforms—many shaped by roofs that met or penetrated the earth—dominated his works. Often (as at the Segel House where he shaped glass and solids similarly) he might fuse the different elements used—concrete, wood, glass, solids, voids, furniture, building, hardscape—into a single interlocking and encompassing set of geometries, eschewing any articulation of the composition. As in a cave, there are only two worlds at play: the fixed shape of the shelter around you and the shifting shape of what is in the view beyond. Internal movement was therefore choreographed around a set of controlled, almost cinematic, changing vistas that not only lay outside the building but came from the perspectives within. In all these late double- or triple-curved concrete shell structures, "you can only see a certain amount of space at the same time and [then] the rest of it appears, and it continues," Lautner said, and, within, the consciousness, "remains." Michael Rotondi spoke of

Segel House, Malibu, California, 1979: study model

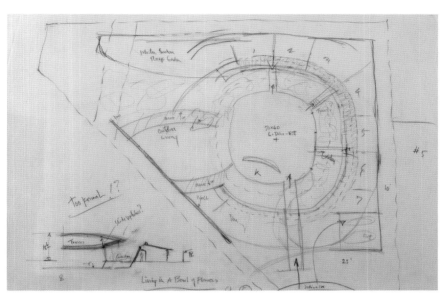

this as Lautner "pushing the limits of perception," and Bruno Zevi said his late work so exaggerated the physicality of space that it placed the body "inside the message."[5]

In all these late works Lautner strove to intensify the exchange between the constancy of a sheltering space and the fluidity of the elements it inhabited. Thus he excited a feeling, as his associate Julia Strickland described it, "of simultaneous safety and expansiveness, groundedness and flight."[6] He saw the Segel House as a "breakthrough" in this direction, saying that Joann Segel, the dance therapist who commissioned it, had precisely understood the idea when she told him that one could stay on the ground and fly at the same time. On the coast, the Segel House was set barely above the high water mark, on the boundary where vegetation ends and rocks and sand begin. Two segments of the same arc intersected like two thick rinds of orange peel, one placed on end and another laid at an angle against it. The collision between the two produced a highly articulated space. "Recessing it in like that," said Lautner, "made it so that when you are in there, you are not only secure in a cave, your orientation is forced up and down the shore." He argued that this duality between security and observation made the building "alive."[7]

Plasticity, absolute fluidity, anageometry, and materials honed to a sheen—these last works of Lautner's are lived-in observatories of nature in its largest sense, human included. In the unbuilt Roven house project (1986), for example, he returned to an abstracted version of his family home, Midgaard, and the mound scheme for Griffith Park; like Silvertop, but inverted, the house served as a comfortable observatory, drawing in a landscape of the stars and sky to make it a chamber between terrestrial and celestial worlds. The Beyer House (1983), in contrast, rejoiced in the obfuscation of the boundary between a world that was dry and sheltered and one that was wild and wet. Fashioning the roof "as a segment of a tilted cylinder" and bringing that curve gently down to the ground behind the shore, he cut the seaward perimeter into a serrated form, "an irregular, informal edge," which had the same rhythm as the rocky point it met.[8]

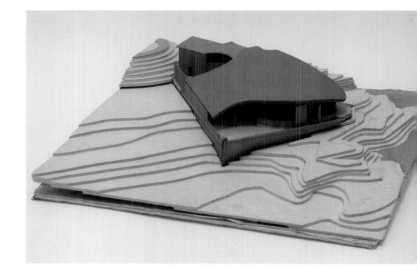

Carted in from the Sierra Nevada mountains, the rock forms around which the living space was organized were similar to those that fell into the ocean beyond. The huge open-plan Malibu Cliff House (1990) completely reversed this idea. Here, Lautner noted, an intensely private, music-mad "bachelor client asked for a whole new world, private, secure, and soundproof." That world was constructed as a secluded echo of the one outside, in which—like the Franklyn and Hope houses—the landscape was simply folded into a huge discrete enclosure. But all remaining distinctions between roof and wall were now forgotten. The house had "thirty-five-foot-high, varying-curving sloping concrete walls enclosing the entire property as living space and becoming the roof of the main house—*all* one Idea."[9]

This sense of containment reached its apogee with two late, unbuilt works on the seashore, for Townsend (1990) and Haagen (1988). The Townsend house project raised

*left*  Beyer House, Malibu, California, 1983: sketch, plan of original scheme
*above*  Beyer House, Malibu, California, 1983: study model

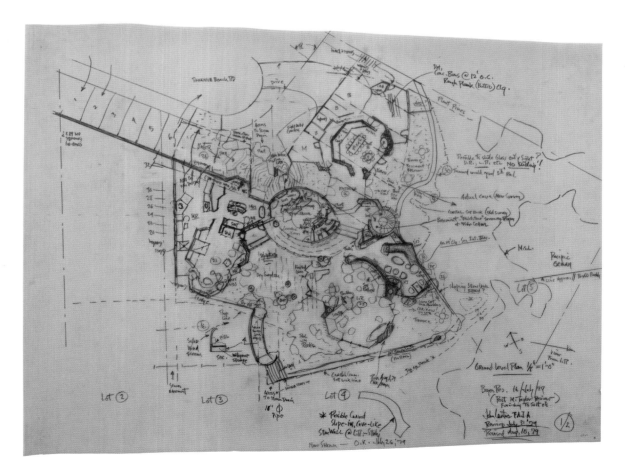

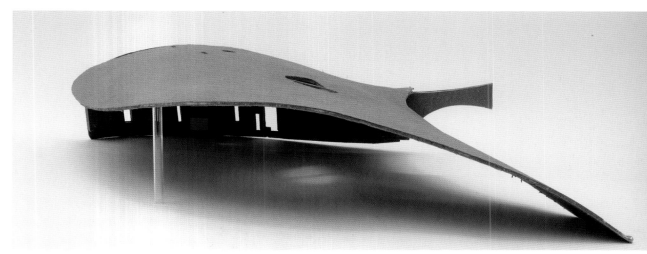

*right* Malibu Cliff House, Malibu, California, 1990:
study model
*below* Malibu Cliff House, Malibu, California, 1990:
sketch, site plan and section

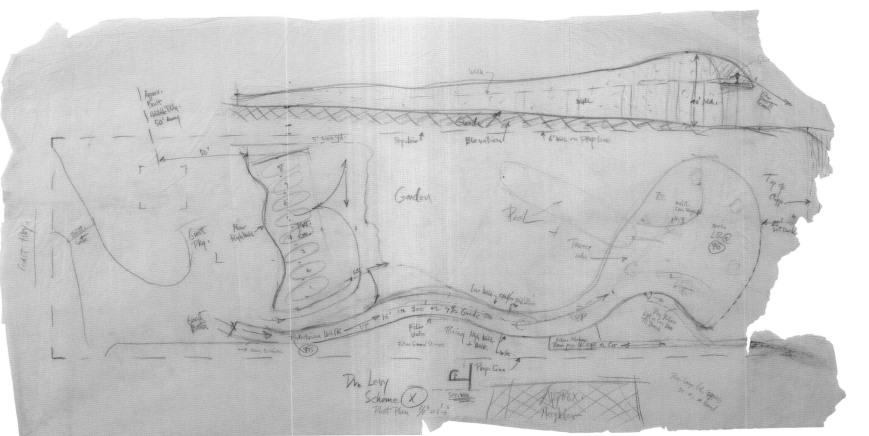

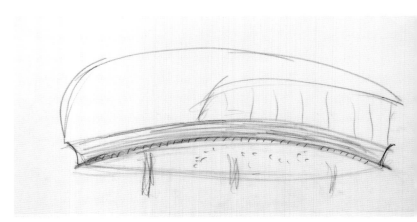

the form of a single well-washed rock above its site, and the latter assembled three equally smooth forms on three shifting levels. In the way they were sited and in the arrangement of their interior spaces, both carried their fluid lines into the openings and closures. The Turner House (1982) in Aspen (which takes a form very close to Lautner's conception, though the materials and construction system were adjusted by the contractor) shows most poetically how this complex new dialogue between the enclosure and its surroundings, in which one is essentially folded into the other, but both allowed to breathe the rhythms of the season, was shaped. Lautner described it as "creating a snowdrift in winter and a grass mound in summer." The exterior settles into its site like a form of nature, and the approach follows a shallow grade that Lautner uses to move one through a densely sculpted enclosure into a panoramic living space that, like a platform under a dome, unfolds the form as a whole with its vistas and swallows the light around it—a progression that leaves the visitor feeling like a butterfly taking flight from its chrysalis.

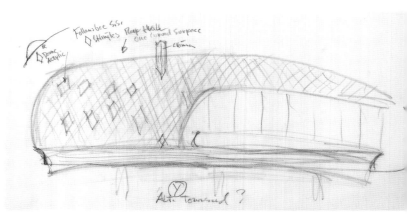

At Turner, we see a suggestion of escape and rebirth. Lautner's next ten years were plagued with pain and distress as illness attacked his mobility. By May 1990, he was in such discomfort that he could not work and even writing had become "next to impossible." As his mobility became ever more troubling, Lautner's isolation intensified. He conceded little; admired less; railed against Los Angeles; ploughed through the massive published set of Le Corbusier sketches and found them "worthless"; assailed Robert Venturi, Michael Graves, and Frank Gehry as slaves to "superficial effect"; attacked Richard Rogers and Norman Foster for offering nothing more than "exposed machinery . . . really no high tech at all." Looking back, he accused Richard Neutra of simply reproducing the same idea for every setting and Bruce Goff of stretching material and structural innovations to inhuman lengths. Paradoxically, now, as his ability to work dwindled, the recognition of his originality grew apace in countless interviews, the first considered critical writing on

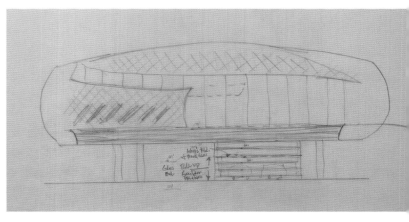

Townsend house project, Malibu, California, 1990: sketch, exterior elevation

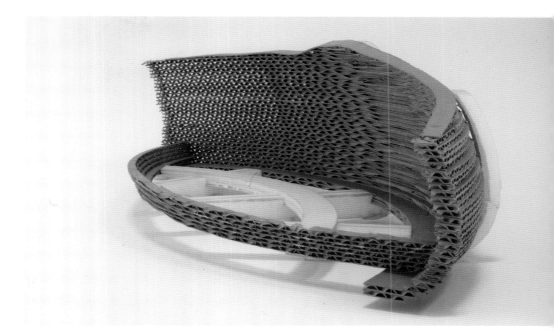

*right* Townsend house project, Malibu, California, 1990:
study model
*below* Haagen beach cabin project, Malibu, California,
1988: sketch, exterior elevation

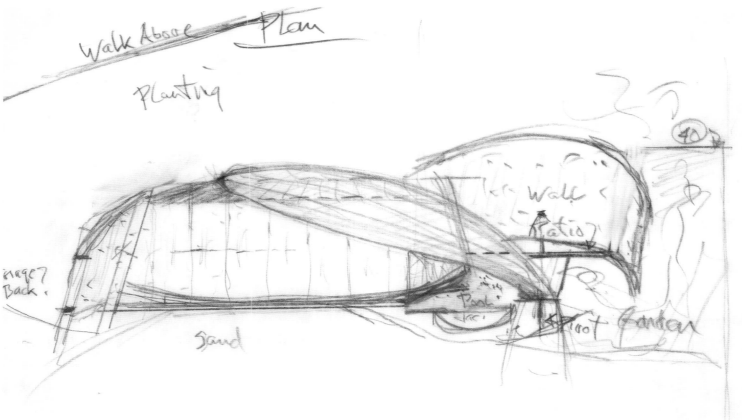

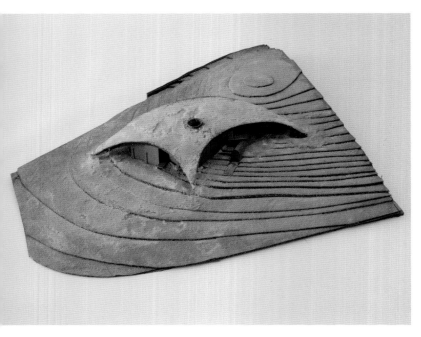

*above* Turner House, Aspen, Colorado, 1982: study model
*below right* Turner House, Aspen, Colorado, 1982: photographed in 2006

his ideas, and a second international traveling exhibition, organized in 1991 and still moving around the galleries of architecture schools at the time of his death. Even his "unfashionably unsavvy . . . humanistic" protests against the vanity of architectural culture and its unreadiness to honor man's stewardship of the earth, said *Progressive Architecture*, now bore "the grim ring of truth."[10]

During what he knew might be his last visit to Midgaard, he sat on the terrace, and there, perched on his billion-year-old rock, looking at the evanescent horizon, he gave his nephew some parting advice. Be faithful, he said, as he had been, to first beliefs. For in spite of the things he could not change, he felt that by remaining loyal to the charge of his childhood, he had opened up as much of the world as he could to a perception of its inherent truths and beauty. "I am," he said, "still a Realist." But, he added, "Change is the only Reality."

### New Patterns for Living

1 *California Designs* 1, no. 1 (August 1947): 16.
2 "Roof Structures by John Lautner," *Arts and Architecture* 65 (June 1948): 36–37.
3 Ibid.
4 *John Lautner Architect: Exhibits by Philip B. Welch* [c. 1950, privately printed; copy in LFA]
5 Ibid.
6 "John Lautner's Houses Take All Hollywood As A Stage," *House and Home*, February 1952: 89–91. [hereafter cited as "John Lautner's Houses . . ."]
7 Ibid.
8 Escher, "Lautner: Tribute," 23.
9 Quoted in *Progressive Architecture* (December 1966): 93.
10 "Circles for the Hillside, Circles for the Beach," *Interiors and Industrial Design* 109 (January 1950): 98–99.
11 *Southwest Builder and Contractor*, 23 June 1950: 18–19, p.18.

### Social Space in the Mobile City

1 "John Lautner's Houses . . ."
    *See also* Betty Peppis, "Houses in the Hills," *New York Times Magazine*, 5 August 1951; Frederick Arden Pawley, "Motels," *Architectural Record* 107, March 1950: 122–131; "Drive-Ins, Banks, Theaters, Restaurants—Building Types Study 164," *Architectural Record* 108, August 1950: 131–53; Lautner Project Descriptions and Notes. Client Files (JLF); correspondence of Lautner with Peter Blake (*Architectural Forum*) and George Sanderson (*Progressive Architecture*), 1947–48 (JLF); Esther McCoy, "West Coast Architects V: John Lautner," *Arts and Architecture* 82, August 1965: 22–27 [hereafter cited as McCoy, "West Coast Architects"]

### Sensing the Terrain

All the architect's quoted statements and explanations are from Lautner Project Descriptions and Notes (JLF); other information drawn from the promotional brochure for Bubbling Wells Resort (1947) and untitled notes for a biographical statement *c.* 1980 (both LFA); and from an interview with Nancy Pearlman by Nicholas Olsberg, October 2005. See also Dan MacMasters, "The Case For the Circular House," *Los Angeles Examiner Pictorial Living*, 1 February 1959: 4–7 [Hatherall]; John Alden Senning, "Close to Nature," *Los Angeles Examiner Pictorial Living*, 11 December 1960: 24–26 [Pearlman]; McCoy, "West Coast Architects" 1965.

### Concrete and the Continuous Line

1 Kenneth Reiner, *Silvertop* (tour-guide pamphlet, mimeograph), 1960 (JLF).
2 Esther McCoy, guide to the Lautner exhibition at the Schindler House (pamphlet), Los Angeles, 1986: 2–3 (JLF). [hereafter cited as McCoy, Schindler House exhibition, 1986]
3 Louise Foster, letter to John Lautner, 13 November 1969 (JLF).
4 Reese, "Dream House," 1960.
5 Escher, "Lautner: Tribute," 21.
6 Ibid, 13–14.
7 Ibid, 21.
8 Ibid, 19.
    Lautner's discussions of drawing and of concrete and the continuous line are best expressed in a radio interview with Nancy Pearlman, 1989 (recording in JLF), in the interview at Taliesin 1989, and in Whiting, 1988, from which these quotations are taken.

### The Democratic Vista

1 "People Who Live in Flying Saucers . . . ," *New York Times*, 29 April 1961.
2 Walker, *Architecture California*: 43.
3 *Daily Telegraph* (London), 25 May 1961; Wolfe, *Playboy*, 1964: 98.
4 Dominique Rouillard, *Building the Slope: California Hillside Houses, 1920–1960*, trans. of *Construire La Pente . . .*, 1984 (Santa Monica: Hennessy and Ingalls, 1999): 129, 131. [hereafter cited as Rouillard, *Building the Slope*]

5 Jim Killingsworth, "The Story of Alto Capistrano," *Orange County Business* 11, Third Quarter 1968: 45–57.
    See also McCoy, "West Coast Architects"; Guy Zebert and Leonard Malin in Escher, "Lautner: Tribute": 14, 22–23. I have also drawn on the extensive Client Files (JLF) for all three projects, especially notes and correspondence on the Midtown School and Alto Capistrano project and promotional materials and press releases for Chemosphere. Correspondence in Client Files on a project for Kansas City, n.d., *c.* 1962, has been used to obtain an example of Lautner's ideas on urban design.

### Sympathetic and Disappearing Space

1 Rouillard, *Building the Slope*, pp. 125–26.
2 Escher, "Lautner: Tribute," 23.
3 Arthur Mann, "The Architect's Perspective" [interview with John Lautner], *Architectural Digest* 28 (July–August 1971): 74–79, p. 74.
    See also Elizabeth Macmillian, *Beach Houses* (New York: Rizzoli, 1994): 68–69 [hereafter cited as Macmillian, *Beach Houses*]; McCoy, "West Coast Architects"; and on disappearing space *Opus Incertum* 1985. I have also drawn on Whiting 1988, and on Lautner's notes on a student thesis on Mar Brisas (JLF) for this idea of dissolution. Other statements on the projects are drawn from Project Descriptions and Notes (JLF) and especially with regard to Griffith Park from Client Files.

### The Extension of the Senses

1 Beata Inaya, ed., *The Three Worlds of Los Angeles* (USIS, 1974), 3–4, 5, 6, 8.
2 Edgardo Contini to the American Institute of Architects, 7 January 1970 (JLF).
3 McCoy, Schindler House exhibition, 1986.
4 Escher, "Lautner: Tribute," 24.
    Much of the discussion of the music and art that Lautner followed is taken from references in interviews; from notes and speaking notes (especially notes on color, n.d., for a talk to interior designers), in the miscellaneous files of JLF, and on the author's interviews with family, acquaintances, and associates.
5 Both speaking in Bette Jane Cohen, *The Spirit in Architecture*, 1998. Film.
6 Escher, "Lautner: Tribute," 27.
7 Macmillian, *Beach Houses*, 20–21; McCoy, Schindler exhibition, 1986.
8 Ibid.
9 Ibid.
10 Ziva Freeman, "Perspectives: Interview with John Lautner," *Progressive Architecture* (December 1993): 64–67.
    See also Dan Weingarten, "Form and Function: Marquette Native Looks Back . . . ," *Daily Mining Journal* (Marquette, Michigan) 6 September 1991. Statements on the works of this period are found quite widely in interviews, but I have relied mostly on Project Descriptions and Notes, notes and annotations to exhibition catalogs and articles (JLF), Whiting 1988 and *Opus Incertum* 1985, for the conceptual basis of the works. Lautner's opinions on architectural fashions, his most pungent descriptions of Los Angeles, his commentary on his illness and discomfort, and his final words to his nephew are taken from the "chronicles" or guest books of the houses in Three Rivers and Marquette (LFA) and from the Pearlman radio interview 1989 (JLF).

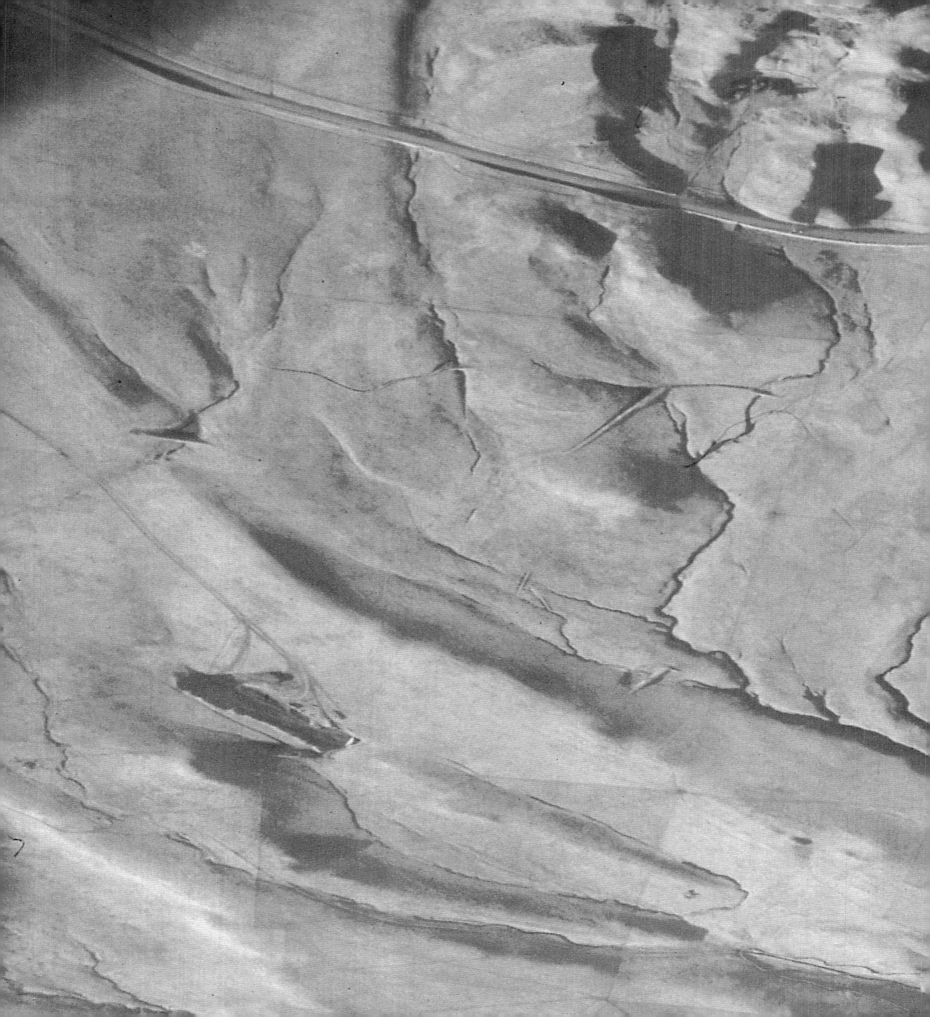

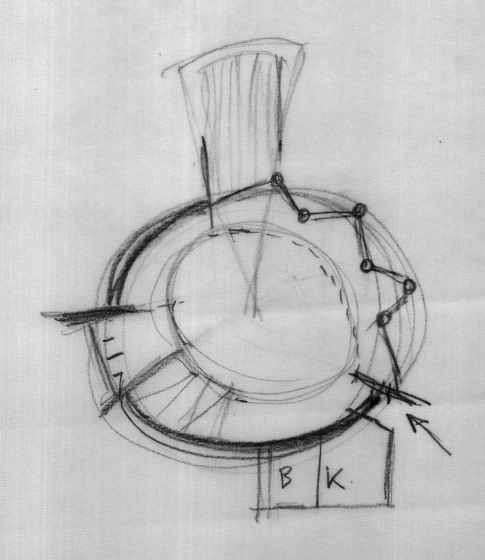

B | K.

W

E

S

Couci
CeDAR

Cars

# 4

# STRUCTURING SPACE

Frank Escher

PEARLMAN MOUNTAIN CABIN

*above, left and far left* Pearlman Mountain Cabin, Idyllwild,
California, 1957
*page 126* Pearlman Mountain Cabin, Idyllwild, California,
1957: sketch, plan of preliminary scheme

# SPACE
## AND
## NATURE

Almost a primitive hut, the modest Pearlman Mountain Cabin in the Idyllwild
arts colony—high on the western slope of Mt. San Jacinto—was built for
accomplished amateur musicians who summered there. A wooden building
in a wooded setting, it is essentially a circular room for music, sitting, cook-
ing, and sleeping. Two thirds of its perimeter is a solid wall with a clerestory of small
rectangular windows. Lined up along this wall are a hearth, a desk for writing, a large window precisely framing an immense oak, two beds, and a tiny kitchen. The other third of
the enclosure opens to the surroundings. Two wings extend out from the body of the house
to frame this opening, one a terrace, the other a bedroom suite. The roof is a fattened
disk with a flat circular center and a tapered edge, folded down to the wall at the back, and
crimped up at the large opening in the front. The construction of the roof is less complicated than its form may suggest: wooden trusses, braced at the center of the house, radiate
out to support it. Across the opening, the roof rests on a row of actual tree trunks. Enormous sheets of glass set directly into these logs form a delicate screen through which one
gazes with wonder at the panorama unfolding beyond.

With these matter-of-fact gestures, Lautner developed an idea of extraordinary beauty: the trunks, both the roof's structure and frames for the windows, echo the trees beyond and unite the space with its expansive, sylvan setting, spatially extending the architecture to the "borrowed landscape." The movement the house allows, from the center towards the edge and back, produces an almost filmic pan, sweeping from the forest, and the enormous boulders strewn about it, up to the mountains and sky. The space, like the later Hatherall, Elrod, and Ernest Lautner houses, or the second Harpel House in Alaska, is circular, but not introspective: like an eye, it focuses on the outside and draws that outside in. The house is set precisely on the edge where the ground begins to tumble down the hill. Solidly on the level ground, even burrowing into it, sits the curved wall, like a cave, to which is fused the delicate glass screen, lifted above the slope on narrow legs that carry the weight of the project down to the concrete foundations. Like a second, unbuilt, project for the Pearlmans in Santa Ana, which reads like the staves of a musical score or the strings of a harp, the cabin suggests a musical analogy in its affinity with the form of a grand piano—a half-open shell sitting on slender legs.

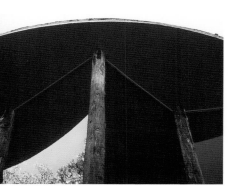

*previous spread* Pearlman Mountain Cabin, Idyllwild, California, 1957: interior view of main space
*far left* Pearlman Mountain Cabin, Idyllwild, California, 1957
*left, middle, and above* Pearlman Mountain Cabin, Idyllwild, California, 1957: exterior views

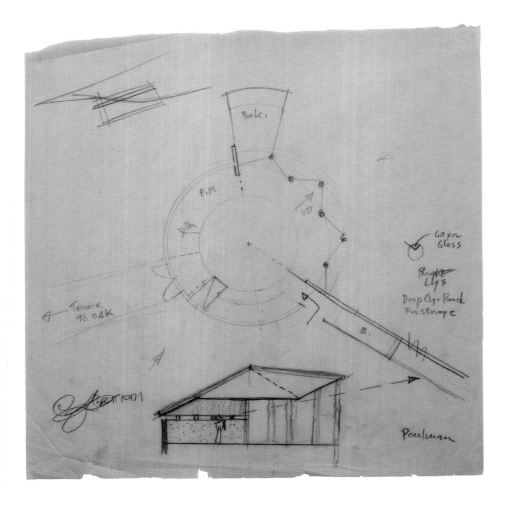

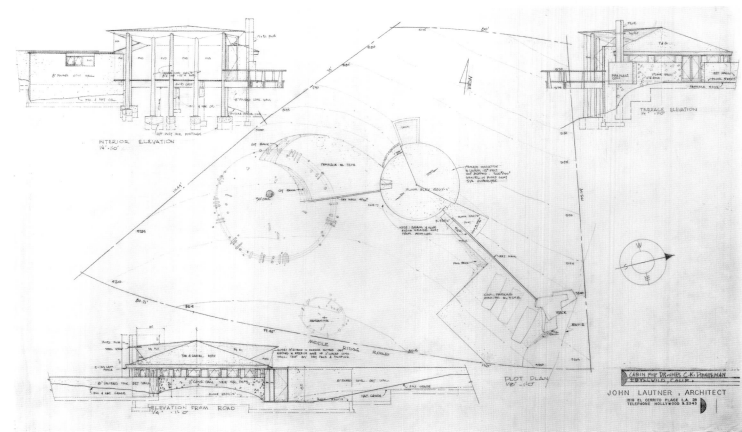

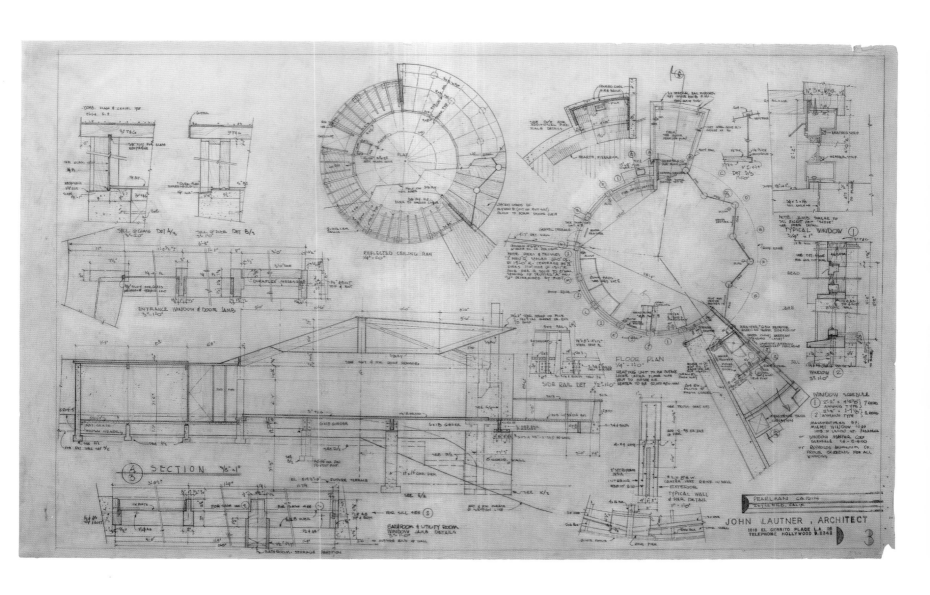

*left top* Pearlman Mountain Cabin, Idyllwild, California,
1957: sketch, plan and section
*left bottom* Pearlman Mountain Cabin, Idyllwild, California,
1957: construction drawing, plan and elevations, site
and exterior
*above* Pearlman Mountain Cabin, Idyllwild, California,
1957: construction drawing, plan, section and details

Mar Brisas, Acapulco, Mexico, 1973: views of the entry

Perched on a hillside high above the bay of Acapulco, the Mar Brisas residence, built seventeen years later, is one of the most extraordinary houses of the twentieth century. The commission had come in July 1970 from a "Mexican Gentleman" who had seen publications of Lautner's Elrod House and was interested in building a resort house with Lautner as architect and Arthur Elrod as interior designer. Walls along the street screen the approach, then a driveway curls down the hill, cuts through, slips out and then back under the roof, which forms an immense arc sweeping out from the hillside. The approach ends in a vast carport, and the house is entered through a monumental bronze door by the German-born artist Mathias Goeritz.

Upon entering, one pauses. The house appears surprisingly small. The short inner edge of the curved roof here is at its lowest point, sloping up towards the perimeter, foreshortening the ceiling and almost entirely removing it from view; at the same time, the bridge that carries one into the house is higher than necessary, lifting one even closer to the ceiling. Not until one moves further into the house does it expand to its dramatic dimensions. Unlike the Pearlman cabin, which is a perch for contemplation, Mar Brisas requires not stillness but movement. Emerging from the precipitous site are an enormous plinth into which the private rooms are tucked and a concrete roof of titanic proportions. Between the new ground that the plinth creates and the roof above it, a large living area opens to the air and view, but bordered and connected by a continuous meandering body of water. Visually and conceptually, this moat, the boundary of the living platform, becomes one with the ocean beyond. The space appears to float between sea and sky.

MAR BRISAS RESIDENCE

Mar Brisas, Acapulco, Mexico, 1973: procession through main space

*above* Mar Brisas, Acapulco, Mexico, 1973: construction drawing, upper-level plan
*right* Mar Brisas, Acapulco, Mexico, 1973: construction drawing, section and details

The decisive concepts were developed early in the design process: Lautner's notes from a first meeting list the program ("master bedroom, five children's rooms, three servants, large open space"), a desire to "Keep Rocks," observe "Minimum grading," and "Collect Day Breeze . . . From Below and Nite [Breeze from] Above."[1] Sketches already show a roof emerging from the hill and hovering over a plinth above the reshaped topography; an upward sloping roof identified as "Disappearing [ceiling]"; and a "Water-Moat Rail," envisaged to frame and focus the views. By January 1971, a contract had been prepared, and Lautner sent a detailed list of "materials necessary to start work." Further sketches begin with a roof reaching out from the mountainside at street level (with a note that the cars "Park on Roof"), and with various structural solutions, including one that anchors it high on the hill, suspended from a support jutting out from the slope. When, at last, the sweeping roof emerges, it is identical to the eventual shape, but proposed as a "Curved Pipe Truss Space Frame." By August, the plans for the "Mountain House" had been sufficiently developed to commence discussions with a structural engineer, and a detailed construction estimate was presented. The costs, in particular the curved pipe truss space frame of the roof, were exorbitant. Weeks of revisions followed: the building area was re-examined, endlessly recalculated, and ultimately reduced, and the decision was made to replace the steel roof: the entire house, plinth and roof, was to be cast in concrete.

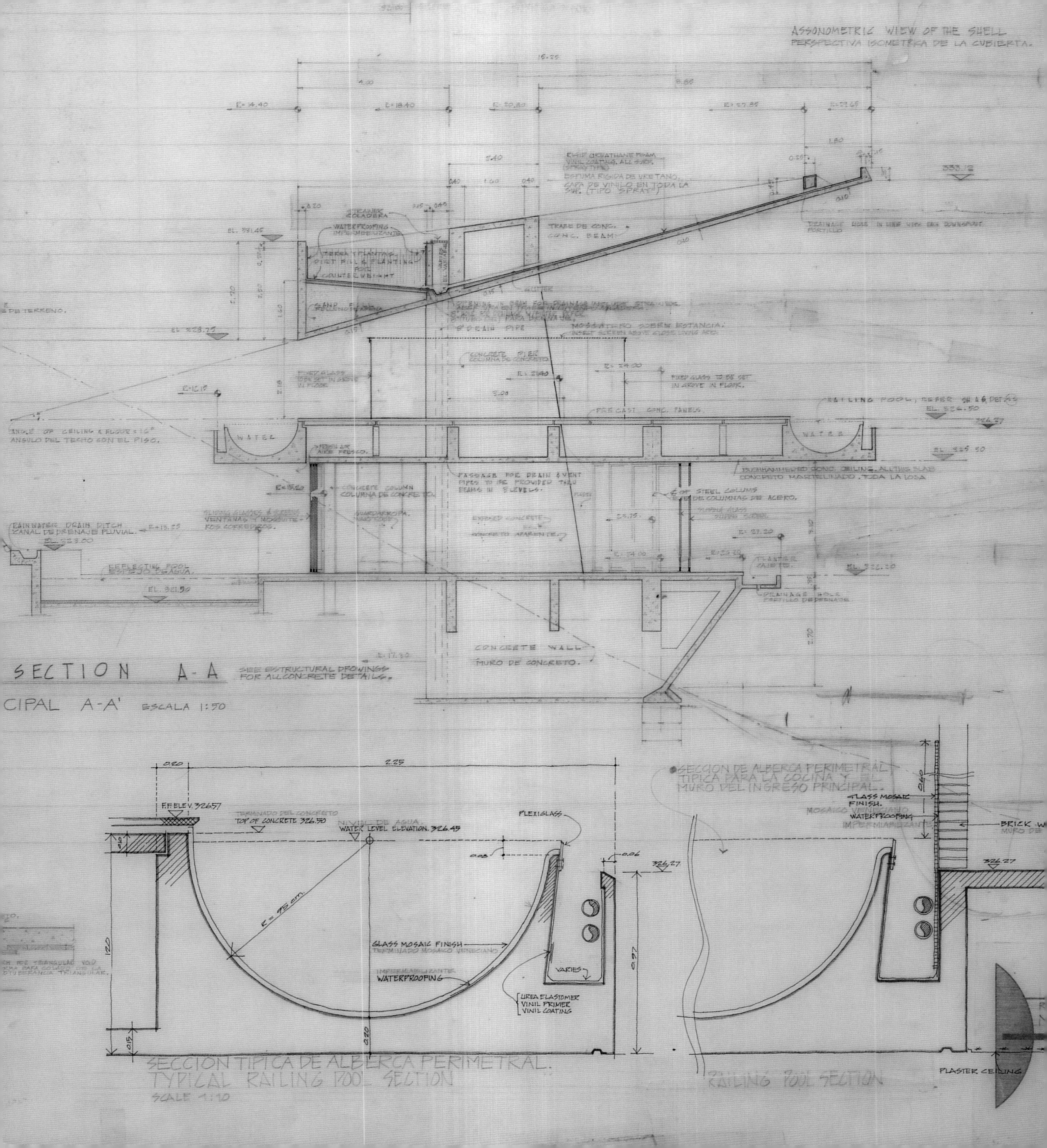

ASSONOMETRIC VIEW OF THE SHELL
PERSPECTIVA ISOMÉTRICA DE LA CUBIERTA.

SECTION  A-A  SEE ESTRUCTURAL DRAWINGS FOR ALL CONCRETE DETAILS.

CIPAL  A-A'  ESCALA 1:50

RIGID URETHANE FOAM
VINIL COATING, ALL OVER
(SPRAY TYPE)
ESPUMA RÍGIDA DE URETANO.
CAPA DE VINILO EN TODA LA
SUP. (TIPO SPRAY)

WATERPROOFING
IMPERMEABILIZANTE

TRABE DE CONC.
CONC. BEAM

DRAINAGE HOSE IN LINE WITH THE DOWNSPOUT

TERRA Y PLANTAS
DIRT FILL & PLANTING
FOR
COUNTERWEIGHT

SAND FILLING

DRAIN PIPE

MOSQUITERO SOBRE ESTANCIA.
INSECT SCREEN ABOVE GLASS LIVING AREA.

CONCRETE PIER
COLUMNA DE CONCRETO

FIXED GLASS TO BE SET
IN GROVE IN FLOOR.

ANGLE OF CEILING & FLOOR = 16°
ANGULO DEL TECHO CON EL PISO.

WATER

FIXED GLASS
TOP SET IN GROVE
IN FLOOR.

AIRE FRESCO

RAILING POOL, UPPER PART & DETAIL
EL. 326.50

WATER

PASSAGE FOR DRAIN & VENT
PIPES TO BE PROVIDED THRU
BEAMS IN 3 LEVELS.

BUSHHAMMERED CONC. CEILING, ALL THIS SLAB
CONCRETO MARTELINADO, TODA LA LOSA.

CONCRETE COLUMN
COLUMNA DE CONCRETO

6" Ø STEEL COLUMN
TUBO DE COLUMNAS DE ACERO.

EXPOSED CONCRETE
CONCRETO APARENTE.

RAIN WATER DRAIN PITCH
CANAL DE DRENAJE PLUVIAL

VENTANAS Y MOSQUITE
FOR CORREDORS

GUARDA ROPA

REFLECTING POOL
ESPEJO DE AGUA.

PLANTER

DRAINAGE HOLE

CONCRETE WALL
MURO DE CONCRETO.

SECCIÓN DE ALBERCA PERIMETRAL
TÍPICA PARA LA COCINA Y
MURO DEL INGRESO PRINCIPAL.

GLASS MOSAIC FINISH.
MOSAICO VENECIANO
WATERPROOFING
IMPERMEABILIZANTE

BRICK WALL
MURO DE

PLEXIGLASS

F.F. ELEV. 326.57

TERMINADO DEL CONCRETO
TOP OF CONCRETE 326.50

NIVEL DE AGUA
WATER LEVEL ELEVATION. 326.45

R = 75 cm.

GLASS MOSAIC FINISH
TERMINADO MOSAICO VENECIANO

IMPERMEABILIZANTE
WATERPROOFING

UREA ELASTOMER
VINIL PRIMER
VINIL COATING

VARIES

SECCIÓN TÍPICA DE ALBERCA PERIMETRAL.
TYPICAL RAILING POOL SECTION

SCALE 1:10

RAILING POOL SECTION

PLASTER CEILING

Mar Brisas, Acapulco, Mexico, 1973: movement to lower level

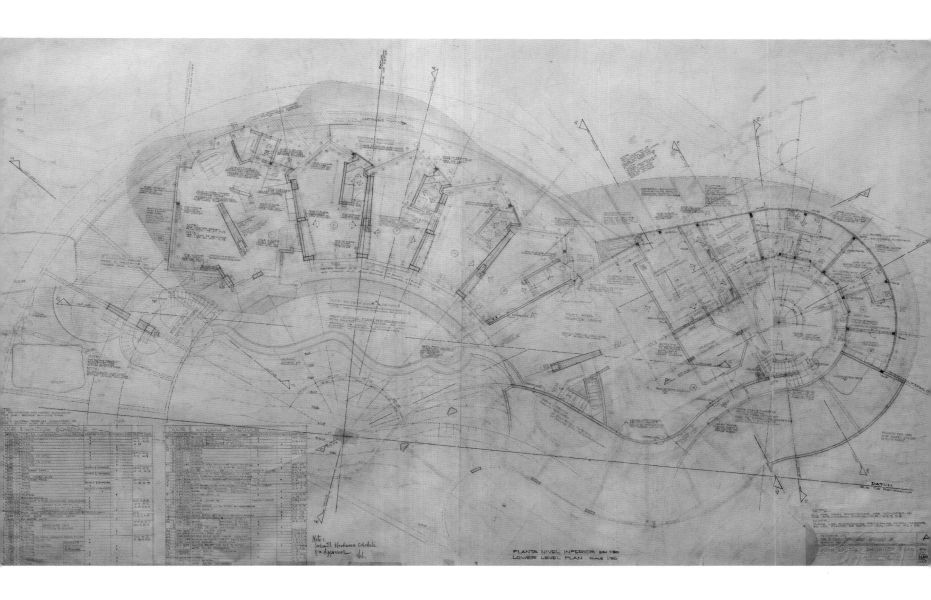

*left* Mar Brisas, Acapulco, Mexico, 1973: exterior views
*above* Mar Brisas, Acapulco, Mexico, 1973: construction
drawing, lower-level plan

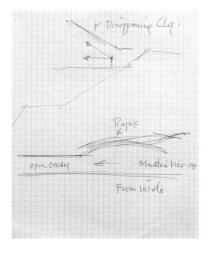

*far left, above, right top, far right bottom* Mar Brisas, Acapulco, Mexico, 1973: views during construction
*left, far right top* Mar Brisas, Acapulco, Mexico, 1973: sketch, sections and preliminary notes
*right middle and bottom* Mar Brisas, Acapulco, Mexico, 1973: sketch, section of roof structure
*following spread* Mar Brisas, Acapulco, Mexico, 1973: main living space

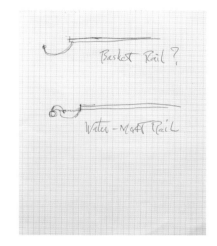

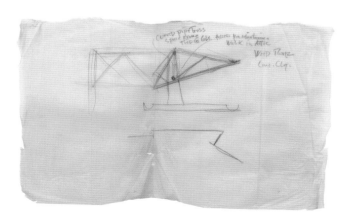

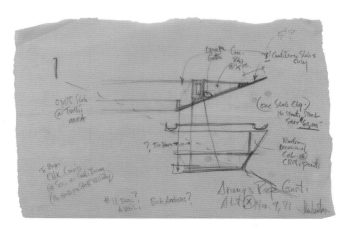

The oddly rustic Pearlman Mountain Cabin and the supremely elegant Mar Brisas house could not appear more different. In many ways, they define the boundaries, or breadth, of Lautner's work. They represent entirely different stages in his career. Their settings—geographically and culturally—could not be more different, nor could their scale, budget, or, more importantly, their construction: the modest Pearlman Mountain Cabin, like many of Lautner's earlier projects, is a simple wood construction, while the Acapulco house is one of his most ambitious concrete forms. They illustrate several ruling principles: a dialogue between form and construction; sculptural firmness and endless space; movement and perceptual shifts. And both, despite the conceptual—and formal—force of their structures, step back to reveal extraordinarily quiet, even contemplative spaces heightened by the rustling sound of the woods, or the din of the ocean and the city below. Even more importantly, the tree trunks of the Pearlman cabin and the moat of the Mar Brisas house serve the same end: they are the natural element that conceptually, visually, and spatially mediates the transition from the architectural space to the surrounding landscapes.

With few exceptions Lautner first conceived his architecture as structured space, then developed it from inside to outside, and only finally shaped it into structural and material solutions. At the same time, his work shows extraordinary sensitivity to the nature of his sites. Lautner's readings are almost seismographic—he sat for a full day on a rock at the Pearlman site absorbing his surroundings before beginning to develop a design. Mar Brisas and Pearlman demonstrate his ability to look beneath the superficial features of a site, and then, through his architectural interventions, make others see what he sees, a careful and precise framing of nature that heightens the perception of one's surroundings, emphasizing what might otherwise go unobserved. In this Lautner is always examining two complementary positions—the sight out to the distant horizon and the absorption of natural forms into the architectural space. The first is exemplified by the spatial explosion of the modest Walstrom House; by Googie's Coffee Shop, where the restaurant's roof opens the space to the hills above; or by the humble Bergren House, where the movement through the house is choreographed towards, and the entire house constructed around, the precisely framed skyward prospect. The precise use of elements of the surroundings to organize and shape architectural space is evident in the first Harpel House, placed at the foot of

*above left* Bergren House, Los Angeles, California, 1953: view to the outside
*below* Wolff House, Los Angeles, California, 1961: study, plan and perspective
*right* Wolff House, Los Angeles, California, 1961: study, interior perspective
*far right* Wolff mountain cabin project, Idyllwild, California, 1975: study model

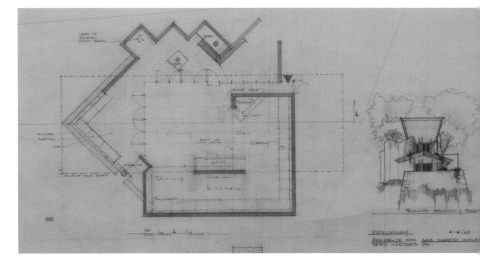

a wall of exposed rock that is then drawn into the dwelling as the back wall of the building; the Beyer House, where the rocky logic of the original site was augmented by hauling in massive boulders to organize the various areas of the main space; or the Wolff mountain cabin project, with its enormous beams placed on top of the massive boulders on the site, allowing the dwelling to freely develop around them.[2]

Between these positions, the far and the near, exists an interesting third: around the habitable space, delicately enclosed with glass, an interstice, a layer of nature or garden is often added, which is then solidly enclosed, expanding the visual experience of the architectural space to this new boundary. By separating the floors from the walls, and the walls from the ceilings, the enclosures do not read as a continuous whole. These gaps are not unlike Wright's open corners breaking up the box, here deftly turned from a vertical to a horizontal position. At the small units of the Desert Hot Springs Motel, the glazed-in living spaces extend past their gardens to the dramatically sculpted "Gunite" wall that establishes the boundary of one's private world. At the Schaffer House, sheets of frameless glass extend the bedrooms out to the private garden, screened by the redwood wall peeling away from the body of the house; and at Wolff, an enormous eucalyptus tree grows between the glass box that is the living space and the sheltering wall. By incorporating these elements into the building, rather than extending the architecture out to nature (as in the work of Richard Neutra or Ludwig Mies van der Rohe), Lautner created unprecedented manifestations of a key principle of Modern architecture: the connection of the architectural space to its surroundings. One can imagine Lautner thinking his spaces out into their surroundings, and feeling those surroundings pulsating back, and finally visualizing the result in the logic of a shaped form, as the complex geometries of his buildings emerging along these intersecting lines from a ground plane. In section, one sees the same careful reading of the land to establish a new ground for the architecture: at times the houses burrow deeply into their sites; or they firmly sit on their sites with topographies moving from the exterior into the houses and out again; or they step and follow lightly the shifting and sloping terrains; or, ultimately, they establish completely new ground, detached and removed, above their sites.

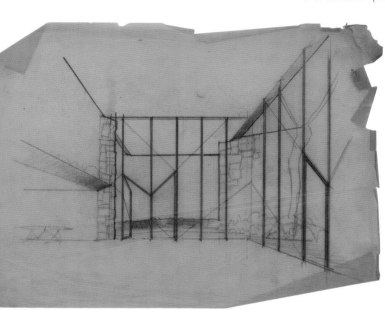

# CONSTRUCTION
# AND
# FORM

Lautner's own contention that every building was absolutely unique and developed "from scratch" (what Claude Levi-Strauss calls the "fruitful illusion" that an artist needs), his deep suspicion of architectural criticism as a discipline (the result of repeated misinterpretation), and his increasing reluctance to explain his own work ("You either get it or you don't") has not helped us to comprehend the underlying structure of his architecture. His buildings, however, are not a string of isolated events but a steady course that results, as Nicholas Olsberg suggests, from "deeply set beliefs." Groups, patterns, and arcs of ideas—sometimes formal, sometimes faint and delicate, sometimes quite bold—emerge and are developed through a series of projects over the years. Lautner was deeply interested in "how things are put together." He had an earnest respect for good, solid craftsmanship, technical skills, and the ability to improvise from these, and he relied greatly on a process of interacting with and manipulating a construction. This would only be possible through a highly developed culture of construction with an interest in such interaction. His architecture, in the best cases, maintained a dialogue with the traditions of the master builder, and possesses an emphatic concern for materials and their means of assembly, from the study of which he saw "form" developing. One is reminded of the term *Baukunst*, which Mies van der Rohe preferred over *Architektur*. It means not the art of building, but building—or constructing—elevated to an art form.

The relationship between Lautner and his builders—in which the skill of the contractor triggered Lautner's architectural, spatial, and formal vision, and Lautner's vision, in turn, pushed the contractor toward new invention—is similar to his relationship with structural engineering. Harvesting to the fullest what the available tools allowed, and imagining what the available tools could not yet do, Lautner constantly experimented with new industrial processes and materials. His formal vocabulary developed as the possibilities of construction technologies opened up, and thus a congruence of construction technology and architectural form characterizes his work. Unlike an entire generation of Southern California architects, who successfully developed an architectural language based on the available means of construction, developing a sort of pop poetry from the local vernacular, Lautner was never interested in exploiting the limits of prevailing construction

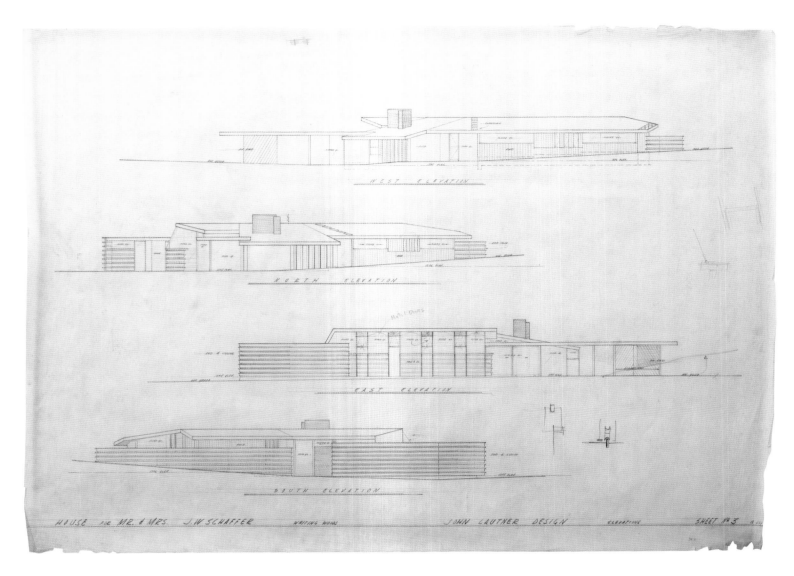

*above* Schaffer House, Montrose, California, 1949: construction drawing, exterior elevations
*left* Schaffer House, Montrose, California, 1949: interior view

practices. His demand for precision set him apart from local building practices. This, at times, led to panicked responses from builders, or shortcuts and restraints from clients responding to growing construction budgets. In the least successful cases, where buildings were completed not as intended or without his watchful involvement, he could not bring himself to accept the result as one of his projects: numerous buildings he designed were thus excised from his official project list.

Lautner's work begins essentially with the technologies of wood and steel, and then—from the early 1960s onward, as Lautner started to get larger commissions—reinforced concrete, a construction technology until then rarely used in residential architecture in Southern California, and which became the muse of his later experiments in plasticity and flow.

Unlike the immediacy of timber construction, where a building is literally put together at its site in a process allowing—in theory—some manipulation, or concrete construction, where wooden molds are assembled on site into which the concrete is poured, much of steel construction—the cutting, drilling, and shaping—occurs off-site.

Schaffer House, Montrose, California, 1949: movement
through and around the house

SCHAFFER HOUSE

The buildings where Lautner used steel not merely structurally but architectonically are few but purposeful: the Dahlstrom House (1949), where a tiny steel-and-glass pavilion is surrounded by a garden that expands the modest space; Googie's, which exploits commercial steel construction, its corrugated steel decking cladding the lightest of steel structures, allowing its roof to fold over the space; the Krause House (1982), whose facade, entirely open to the sea, is developed as a system of diagonal steel braces, and the glass then set into this fractal geometry; and the Lincoln Zephyr Showroom (1948), whose massive steel roof, anchored to the ground in the rear, folds up dramatically to reveal the shiny new cars to the traffic outside.

With its roots in European wood-building traditions, American timber construction had been successfully streamlined and refined, from harvesting, dimensioning, and transporting lumber to reducing costs of construction and, more importantly, to decreasing the dependency on trained craftsmen.

Lautner's first small low-cost residences were built using fairly conventional techniques in raw heavy-cut wood, from which astonishing spatial complexities emerged. The Schaffer House (1949), one of the early masterpieces, appears as a composition of sloping and angling planes of glass and wooden boards, posts, and beams, not because Lautner was interested in this composition per se, but because this was the enclosure for the space he envisioned for this site. Space—and structure—delicately weaves around the existing oak trees and into the site. The building is carefully thought out and exquisitely constructed, the horizontal wood siding at times solid, at times alternating with bands of glass, and, finally, peeling off completely from the house to create small private gardens.

From the mid-1950s on, Lautner began to bend and shape wood, working increasingly with prefabricated, glue-laminated wood technologies ("glulam"). In the small office structure for Paul Speer, the builder of many of Lautner's early projects, gently curving glue-laminated beams—used here for the first time—lift the roof of the walls

*above* Henry's Restaurant, Pomona, California, 1957: exterior view
*below* Speer Contractors Office Building, Los Angeles, California, 1956: interior view
*above right* Henry's Restaurant, Pomona, California, 1957: view of roof structure
*below right* Henry's Restaurant, Pomona, California, 1957: construction drawing, plan, elevation, and details

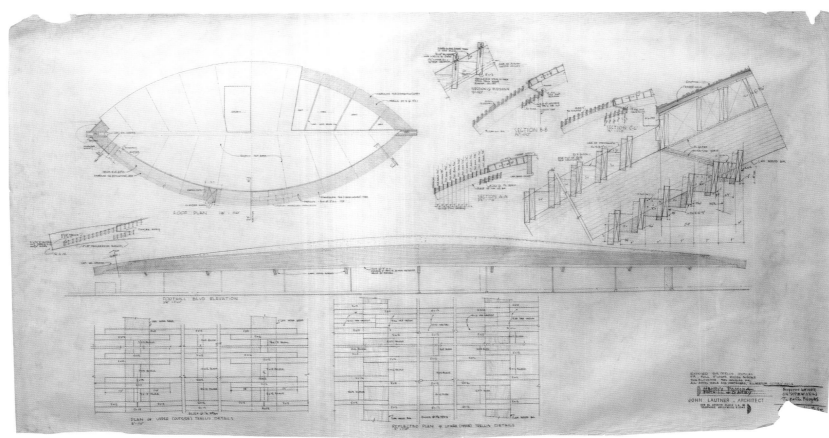

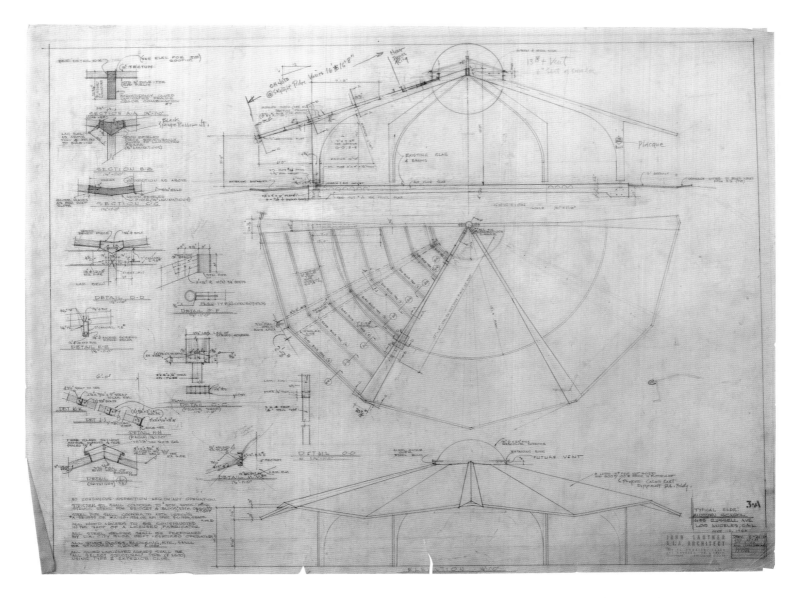

to reveal a sliver of mountain view. The roof of Henry's Restaurant in Pomona resembles the structure of an upturned boat with a keel and ribs; and in the prefabricated roof structures of the Midtown School (1960), the arced supports are tied together with a steel tension ring, allowing complete flexibility to use and combine the units.

*above* Midtown School, Los Angeles, California, 1960:
construction drawing, roof structure plan, section, and elevation
*right* Midtown School, Los Angeles, California, 1960:
view of roof structure
*far right* Midtown School, Los Angeles, California, 1960: study,
plan of roof structure

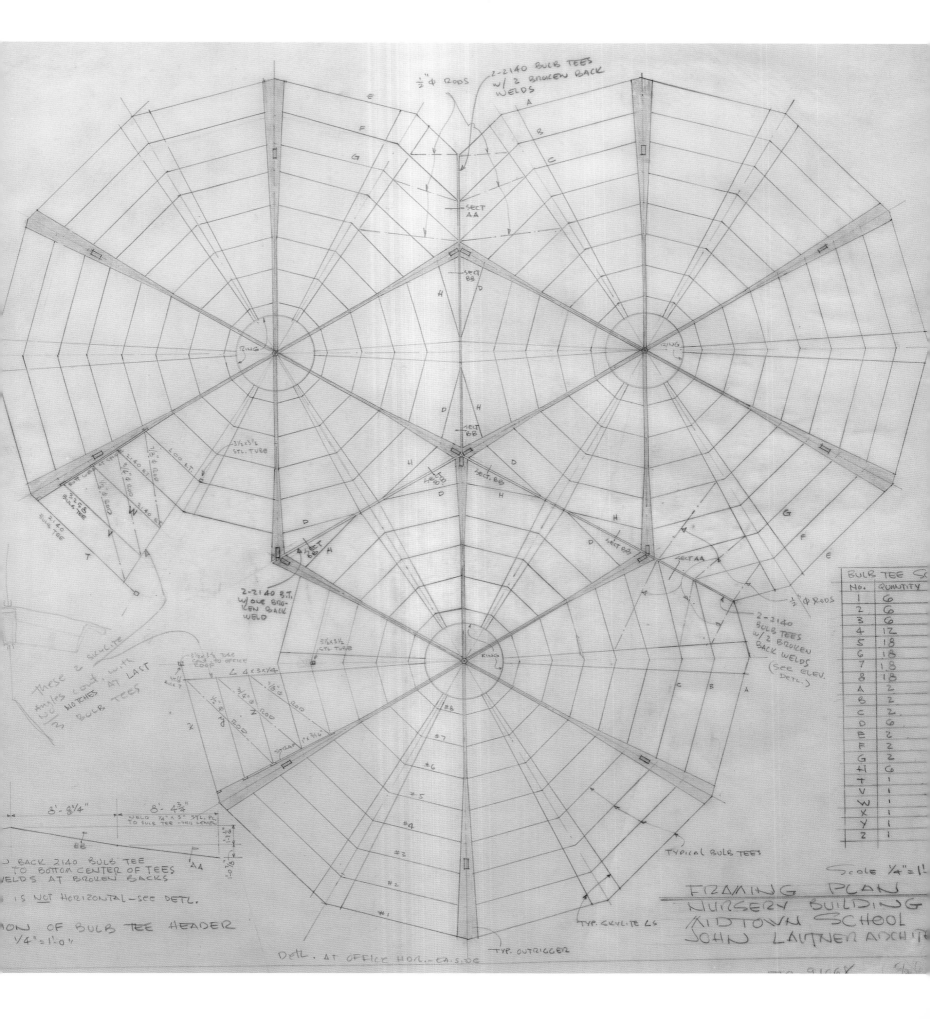

FRAMING PLAN
NURSERY BUILDING
MIDTOWN SCHOOL
JOHN LAUTNER ARCHITECT

Scale ¼" = 1'

| BULB TEE S... | |
|---|---|
| NO. | QUANTITY |
| 1 | 6 |
| 2 | 6 |
| 3 | 6 |
| 4 | 12 |
| 5 | 18 |
| 6 | 18 |
| 7 | 18 |
| 8 | 18 |
| A | 2 |
| B | 2 |
| C | 2 |
| D | 6 |
| E | 2 |
| F | 2 |
| G | 2 |
| H | 6 |
| T | 1 |
| V | 1 |
| W | 1 |
| X | 1 |
| Y | 1 |
| Z | 1 |

A long, narrow road winds from the city up the hills through the tight Beverly Glen canyon to the Walstrom House (1969). Halfway to the top a tighter side canyon opens up and leads to a short, steep driveway. One parks at the bottom of the hill, clambers up the path to the house, enters, and moves up the ramp to the main space. The view here is of the open sky.

After his first visit to the steep site—Lautner crawled through the bushes to reach the top of the property—he quickly developed three different schemes: a large tube, with platforms floating within, angled on the slope; a pair of cylinders, studied in some detail and later abandoned; and a tower, which was ultimately built. The path, the movement up the slope, was carefully drawn and studied. The simple structure of the building consists of two enormous triangles: a tall vertical support rises from the bottom of the hill, a diagonal brace secures this to the hill, and a concrete grade beam connects the two glulam beams below ground. These two triangles, and the downhill-facing wall, are perpendicular to each other, but the path crosses this arrangement at a slight angle, creating a trapezoidal footprint. This small distortion sets off a surprising geometry: the wooden structure of the roof converges slightly from one side to the other, the two side walls are different lengths and end at varying heights on the hill, as the ramp continues through the house. This ramp, again, separates from the exterior walls the floor of the living space, which then is organized around two volumes—an open kitchen and a library, the latter enclosing a small bath within and supporting an open loft above. The planar geometries of the carpentry and cabinetry echo the radical geometry of the whole and relate this small wooden house to Lautner's earliest work. The nexus of the house is its entry. Here, one immediately grasps the house both in plan—to the left a few steps lead down to the bedrooms, straight ahead the ramp slopes up to the main level—and in section—the wooden construction is lifted off the ground and slipped into this interstice is a private, enclosed garden.

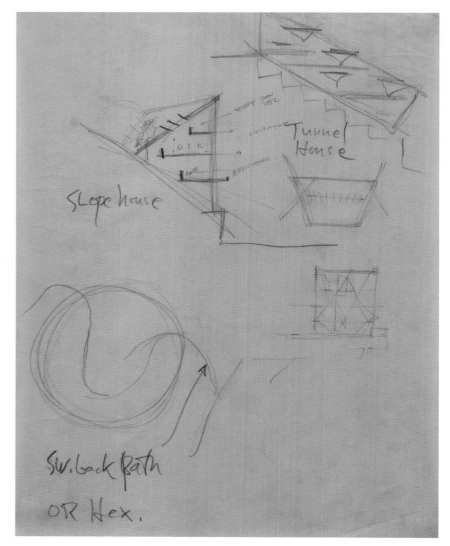

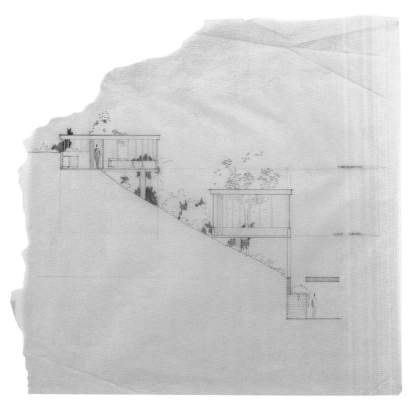

*left* Walstrom House, Los Angeles, California, 1969: sketch,
sections of preliminary schemes
*above* Walstrom House, Los Angeles, California, 1969:
study, section
*right* Walstrom House, Los Angeles, California, 1969:
sketch, site plan
*below right* Walstrom House, Los Angeles, California, 1969:
study, section and circulation

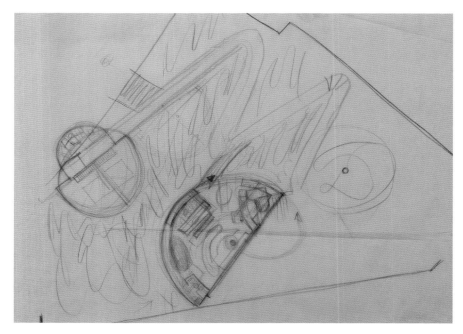

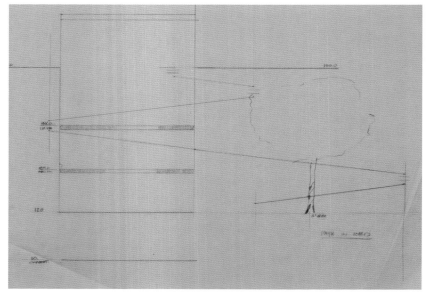

WALSTROM HOUSE

*above and right* Walstrom House, Los Angeles, California, 1969
*far right* Walstrom House, Los Angeles, California, 1969: entry
ramp to main interior space

Walstrom House, Los Angeles, California, 1969: interior
view of main space

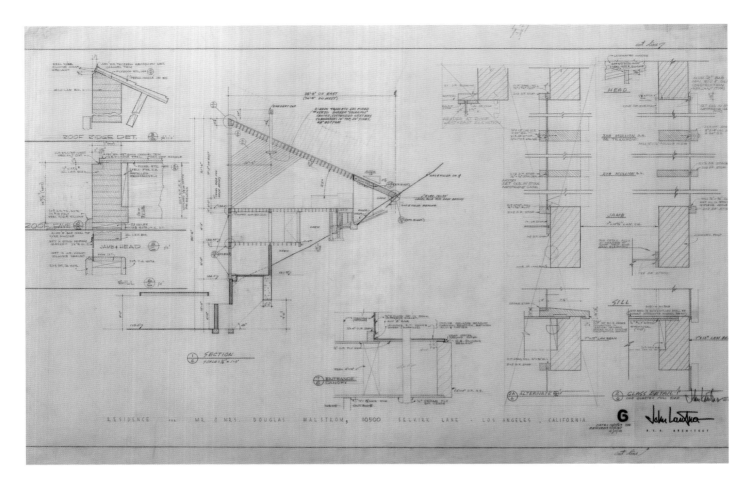

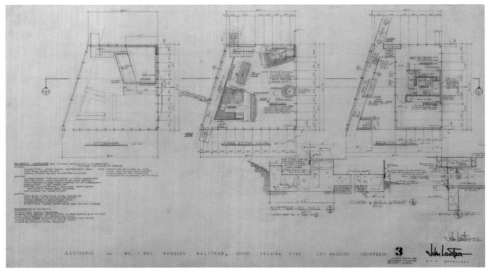

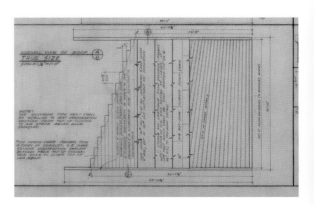

*top* Walstrom House, Los Angeles, California, 1969:
construction drawing, section and details
*above left* Walstrom House, Los Angeles, California, 1969:
construction drawing, upper-, main-, and lower-level plans
*above right* Walstrom House, Los Angeles, California, 1969:
construction drawing, framing and structural engineering plan
*right* Walstrom House, Los Angeles, California, 1969: view
of exterior and garden beneath the house

Chemosphere, Los Angeles, California, 1960: views during construction

Perched on a single concrete column, the Chemosphere is a brilliant structural solution to a precipitous site—a site at first considered to be unbuildable. Like a tree, the structure sprouts from the hill. Built in 1960, it is not only one of Lautner's most important projects, but is one of the best-known houses of Los Angeles, a building that represents the optimism of its time and place as much as the architect's genius.

The nineteen-foot-diameter, three-foot-thick circular concrete foundation pad is embedded into the bedrock and covered with four feet of compacted soil. A five-foot-diameter, twenty-nine-foot-high concrete column, with a two-foot hollow for water supply and sewer, carries the roughly sixty-foot-diameter octagonal platform of steel and wood. Eight steel beams radiate from the center and are supported on eight diagonal steel braces. Short steel pieces extend these braces past the floor level to the underside of the window. Eight curved glue-laminated beams, supported on the extended braces and tied at the center of the house to a steel compression ring, form the structure of the roof—similar to the structure developed around that time, and produced by the same manufacturer, for the roof of the Midtown School (1960). The saw-cut roof joists are precisely set into notches in the glulam beams, their spacing depending on their spans: wider spacing for the shorter spans (closer to the center of the house), tighter spacing for the longer spans (at the edge of the roof, giving lateral support to the glulam beams where the roof curves and precisely defining the edge of the roof). None of the interior walls are load bearing. At the center, above the fireplace, is a skylight, balancing the light from the perimeter. A large living, dining, and kitchen area occupies roughly one half of the house, facing north and a view of the sprawling suburbs. The other half, facing the hill, accommodates three bedrooms, a laundry room, and two bathrooms. It is a house suspended between the "wilderness" and the "city." The current owner recalls watching an adventurous raccoon ambling around the wide window sills and pressing its nose against the office window,

CHEMOSPHERE

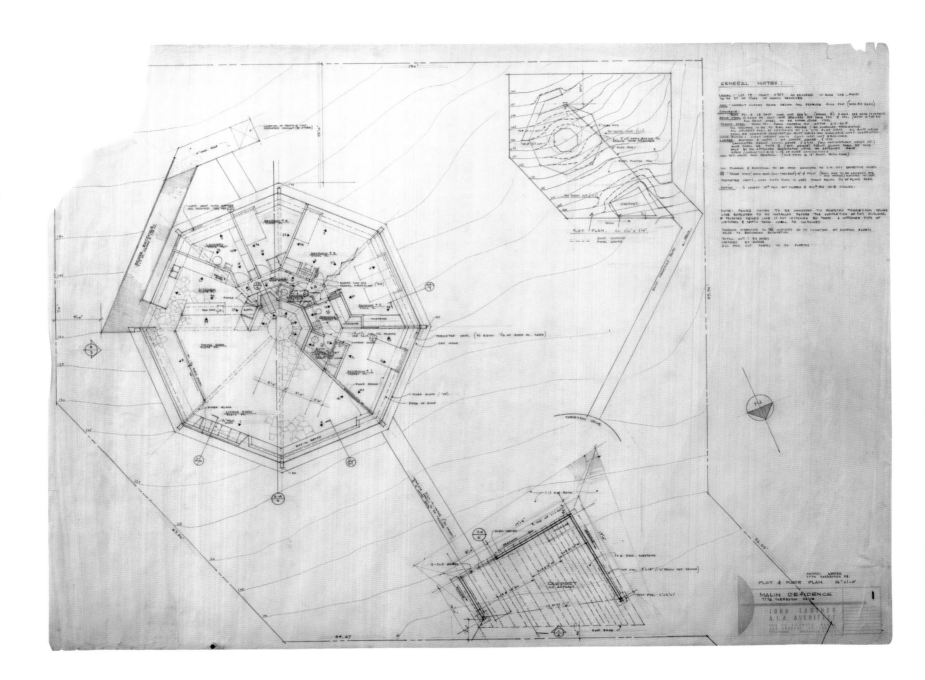

*above* Chemosphere, Los Angeles, California, 1960:
construction drawing, plan
*right* Chemosphere, Los Angeles, California, 1960:
construction drawing, elevation, and section

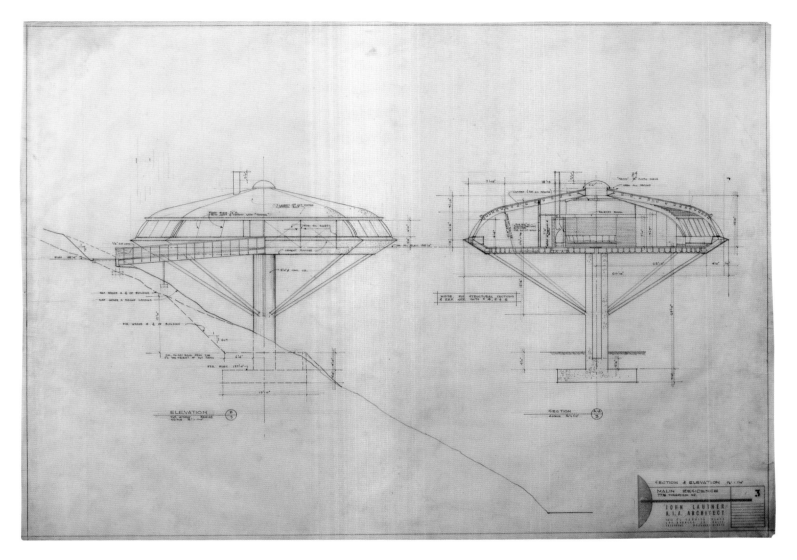

while the original owner remembers stepping into his living room one morning to find an entire human family on his balcony, peering into his house.

Lautner designed the house for a young aerospace engineer, Leonard Malin, and his family. Malin had acquired the land from his father-in-law, who lived on the street below the site, and there he met Lautner, who had completed the nearby Harpel House in 1956. Malin was personally involved with developing details, mechanical systems, and construction. In addition, the house was sponsored by Southern California Gas (which supplied all appliances, heating, and cooling units in exchange for the right to use the house for advertising), and the Chem Seal Corporation, manufacturers of bonding, sealing, and coating compounds used in the aerospace industry, and applied in the construction. For weeks, Lautner climbed around the hill, sitting and gazing at the view. At night only the glow of a cigarette would be visible. He developed four schemes, but, unsatisfied, continued for weeks to brood—meanwhile, the client had given instructions to proceed with one of them and waited impatiently. Lautner, the story goes, returned with his project architect, Guy Zebert, to look at "that lousy lot," stood at the bottom of the hill for a while, shook his head,

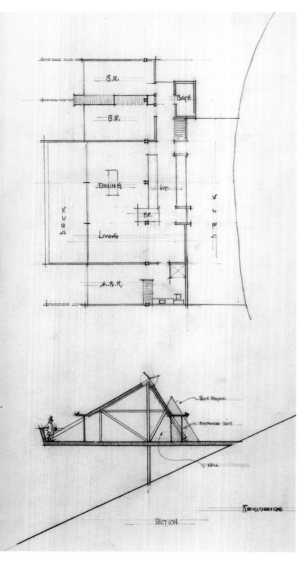

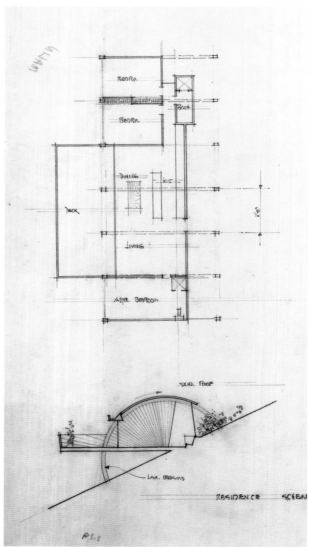

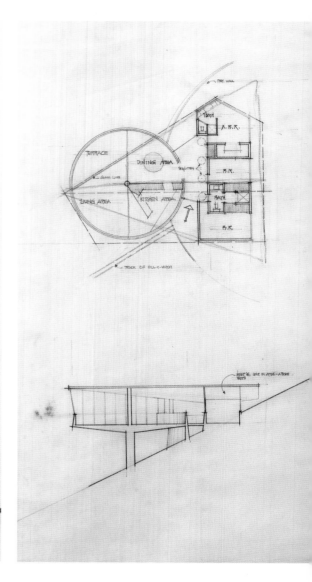

*previous spread* Chemosphere, Los Angeles, California,
1960: view of the city
*above* Chemosphere, Los Angeles, California, 1960: study,
plans, and sections of preliminary schemes

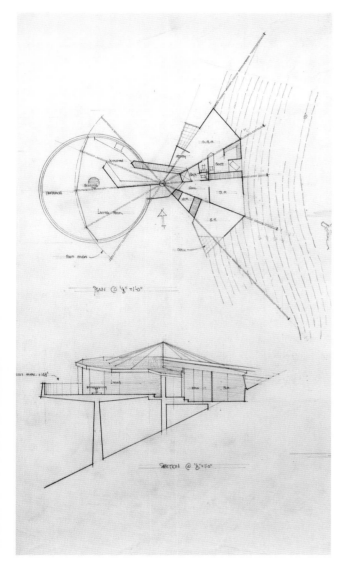

and declared "there is no lot." He then pulled out an envelope from his pocket and drew the basic scheme for the house: a diagonal line indicating the slope, a horizontal line for the floor, a vertical one connecting both, and a curved line roofing over his platform. He then handed the sketch to Zebert with the instructions to "finish the drawings." Of the four schemes Lautner initially developed, however, two were straightforward linear arrangements along the hill: one with a central row of supports, one with structural arcs stapling the house to its site. In the other two schemes, Lautner had already begun to move parts of the program off the hill and onto a mushroom platform. But it was only with this visit to the site that Lautner thought of simply placing the entire house on one large, freestanding structure.

Deeply fascinated by the possibilities of mushroom structures and their economic promise, he had used similar structural concepts on other projects, most unbuilt, beginning in 1948. The only built project with a similar engineering concept was the Sheats "L'Horizon" Apartments (1948) in Westwood, structured in a series of "mushrooms," each made up of a central concrete column supporting a thirty-five-foot-diameter platform of radiating wood joists and held together with a steel tension ring. Following Chemosphere, Lautner continued to apply this structural strategy to similar settings. In the Alto Capistrano development (1963–69), Lautner envisioned entire forests of these structures growing on the hills, leaving the hills untouched. The units would be carried by two supports fused together. An unbuilt private house for Morris Misbin, the developer of the Alto Capistrano scheme, introduced a square variation on this idea, which is further developed in the Peters house project (1968): here mushrooms, stacked as in the Sheats Apartments, reduce the structure of the house to its most elegant minimum. Floor-to-ceiling glass walls enclose what would have been an extraordinary building. The last exploration of this structural idea, where central symmetry is required by gravity, occurs in the last proposed scheme for Alto Capistrano, with platforms assembled here from precast coffered slabs.

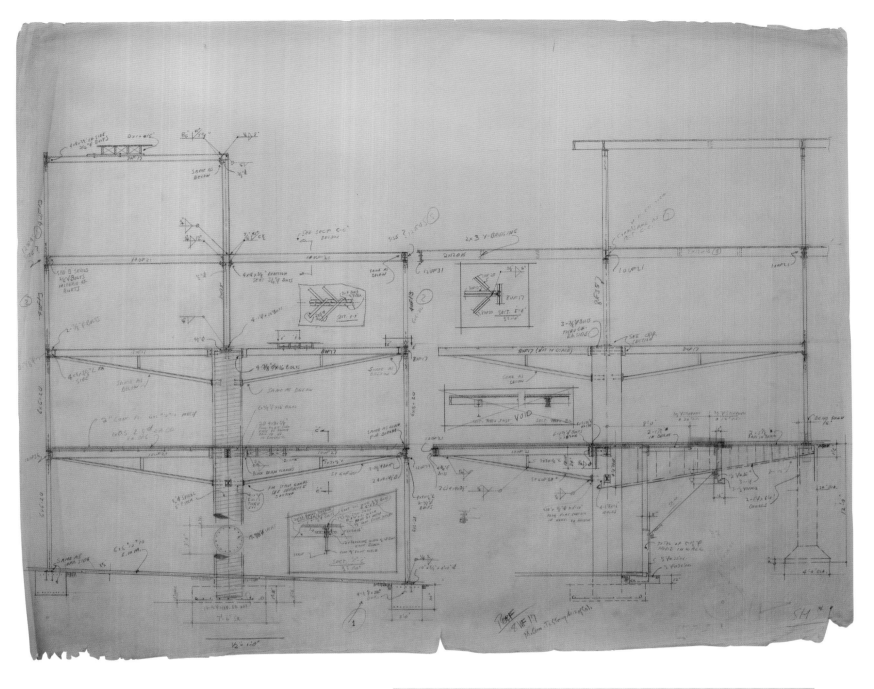

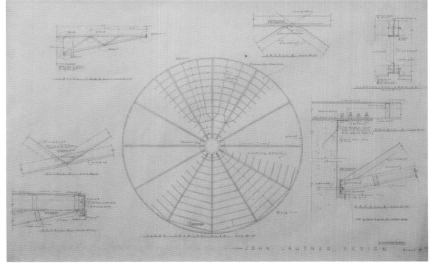

*above* "L'Horizon" Apartments, Los Angeles, California, 1948:
study, section of structure
*right* Abbot apartments project, Los Angeles, California, 1948:
construction drawing, plan, and details for structure and framing
*far right* "L'Horizon" Apartments, Los Angeles, California, 1948:
views during construction

SHEATS "L'HORIZON"
APARTMENT BUILDING

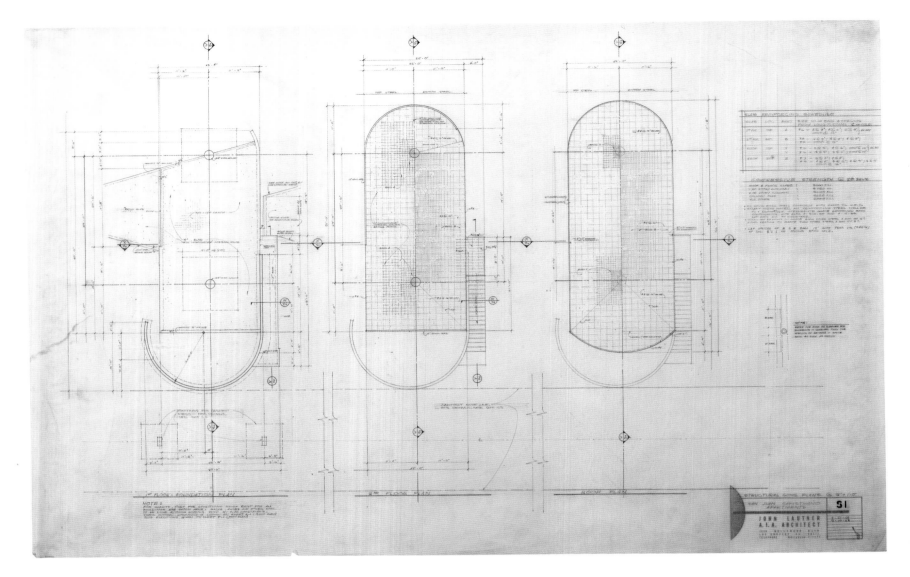

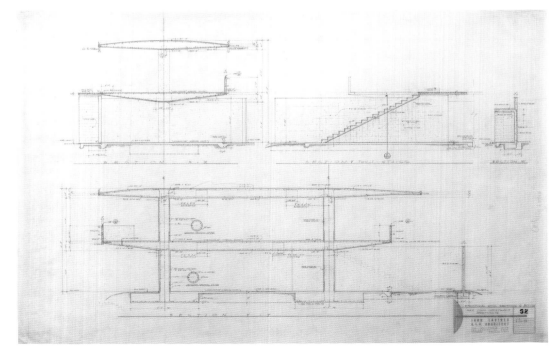

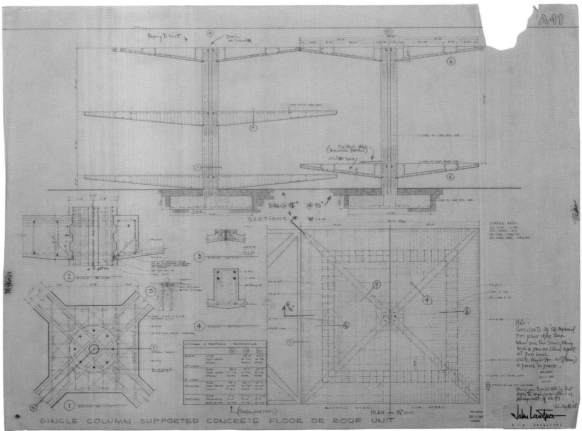

*left top* Alto Capistrano project, San Juan Capistrano, California, 1963–69: construction drawing, plan

*left* Alto Capistrano project, San Juan Capistrano, California, 1963–69: construction drawing, section of structural system

*above* Peters house project, Thousand Oaks, California, 1968: study model

*right* Misbin house project, Los Angeles, California, 1968: construction drawing, section, and details of structure

# INVENTION
## AND
### ENGINEERING

The dialectic between form and technology, a defining concept in understanding any cultural artifact, raises the question of whether the artist's vision pushes technological developments or technological developments propel the artist's vision. It is difficult to imagine Lautner's work outside the context of twentieth-century structural engineering. Much like his relationship with his builders, his contact with structural engineers led to a dialogue in which their abilities inspired him and his architectural visions challenged them. As the field of structural engineering slowly flowed away from symmetry towards fluid and undulating shapes, Lautner increasingly explored highly complex geometries: surface, form, and structure melted together, and more importantly, space and structure intertwined. Like the relationship between a glacier and a rock, one forms the other. What astonishes is not simply the elegance of the forms he produces, but the elegance of the thinking that informs them. Lautner's work in concrete, as with timber construction, describes a development—arcing from simple symmetrical structural concepts, from flat beams and slabs, to shapes of single curvature, and, finally, to double curves, asymmetrical systems, and forms of enormous geometrical complexity. To achieve this, Lautner drew on an understanding of engineering that was not simply intuitive but thoroughly educated: he prepared structural calculations himself on many smaller projects—such as the Bergren House (1953)—and at times would go as far as claiming to have engineered projects—like the Malibu Cliff House (1990)—entirely himself.[3]

Robert Maillart, the Swiss engineer, greatly influenced structural engineering in the first part of the twentieth century, making possible Lautner's later explorations. His Alpine bridges, many utterly beautiful, were published and exhibited widely, including, in 1947, at the Museum of Modern Art (MoMA) in New York.[4] But his work on spatial structures may be even more influential. In 1908, he developed a system that allowed a fluid but rigid connection between a vertical support and a horizontal slab, by organically flaring out the posts to meet the slab. This idea, the "mushroom slab," simplified and made more economical the building of many large concrete structures, including Wright's Johnson Wax Administration Center (1936), whose construction Lautner had observed.

Lautner collaborated first with structural engineer Edgardo Contini, who in 1952 published an article on Maillart's concrete bridges. Contini, the son of an engineer and grandson of a builder from Ferrara, was forced, as a Jew, to leave Italy for the United States in 1938, settling after wartime military service in Los Angeles, where he became

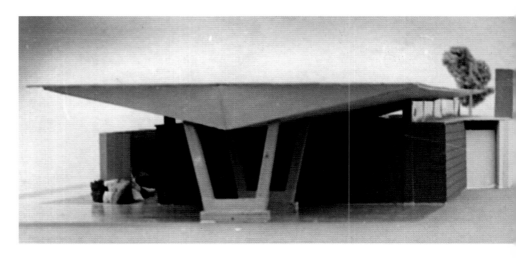

one of the principal designers of the Crestwood Hills housing cooperative. At the same time Contini was working with Lautner on projects that relaunched Lautner's career after the war: the Valley Escrow Company building, the prefabricated steel roof structure for the Lincoln Zephyr Showroom (1948) in Glendale, the guesthouse for Arthur Eisele (1946); and the first projects with mushroom supports—the Stiff and Ross houses, the Abbot apartments project, and most likely the Ferber house project and Sheats Apartments (all 1948).

Contini also worked on Lautner's critical explorations of independent roof structures for single-family dwellings, which allowed many of the clients of these small projects to build the walls beneath their roofs themselves. Starting in 1946 with the Mauer House (and a similar structure used for the Eisele Guesthouse), the roof structure is developed as a series of elegant, L-shaped plywood box-beams. The strong asymmetry of the structures moves the center of gravity out of the central space to one side, and allows the structure to dissolve at the other end, where the box beams rest on slender steel posts. In the Gantvoort House (1947), the bow-trusses, thickened at the center to resist the structural loads, rest on delicate steel posts, slanted inwards to resist both vertical and lateral (i.e. seismic) forces; while the concave upper bow of the truss and the curved ceiling gently enclose and shelter the domestic space, the convex lower bow allows this interior space to flow up to the sky, setting up a quiet dialogue between the enclosed and the open. A similar roof structure, in timber, was developed for an unbuilt house for Jules Salkin (1948). Here a shallow inverted triangular truss opens the space to the sky. Sitting on a series of paired sloped wooden supports, the roof, tapering to a subtle thin edge, allows the dwelling beneath to develop freely into discrete private spaces that interlock with its garden enclosure. The roof systems developed by Contini and Lautner for the Carling, Polin, and Jacobsen houses (all 1947) all used a hexagonal steel and timber frame, suspended from three tapered steel trusses. The Carling House, in particular, takes full advantage of this ingenious structure: none of the walls are load-bearing; they slide and pivot, and they turn the house into a pavilion open to the world.

This early collaboration with Contini resonates through the next twenty years of Lautner's work. While he worked with other structural engineers on critical elements of many projects—Richard Bradshaw, Barney Cardan, and John Porterfield—it is clear that it was Lautner himself who proposed the structural strategies, often greatly extending ideas, like the mushroom structures at Chemosphere and Alto Capistrano, first examined with Contini.

*left* Mauer House, Los Angeles, California, 1946: roof construction
*below left* Eisele Guesthouse, Los Angeles, California, 1946: view of exterior
*above right* Salkin house project, Los Angeles, California, 1948: study model

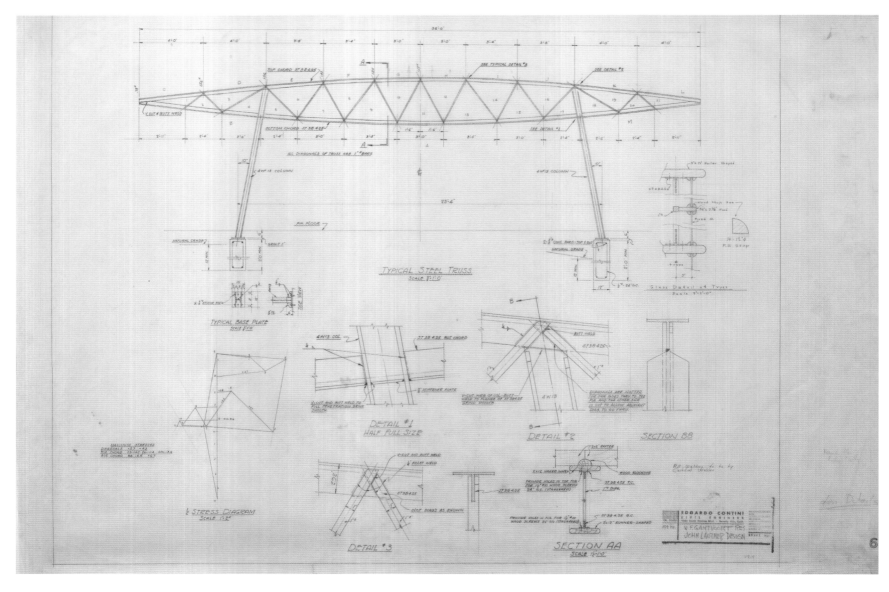

TYPICAL STEEL TRUSS

# GANTVOORT HOUSE

*left top* Gantvoort House, Flintridge, California, 1947:
construction drawing, engineering section and details
*left bottom and above* Gantvoort House, Flintridge,
California, 1947: views of roof during construction
*left* Gantvoort House, Flintridge, California, 1947:
exterior view

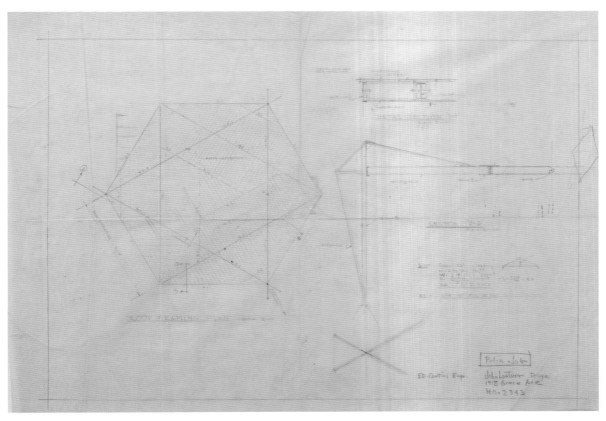

*left* Jacobsen House, Los Angeles, California, 1947: view
during construction of roof
*above* Polin House, Los Angeles, California, 1947:
construction drawing, roof structure plan, section, and details
*right* Carling House, Los Angeles, California, 1947: view
during construction of roof

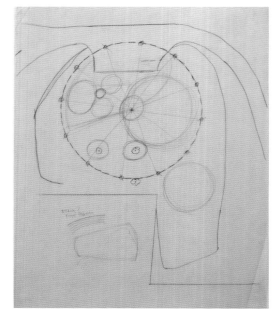

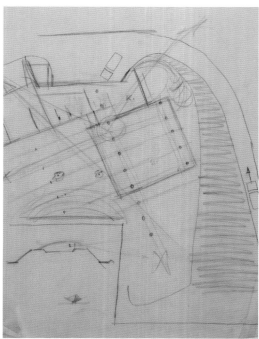

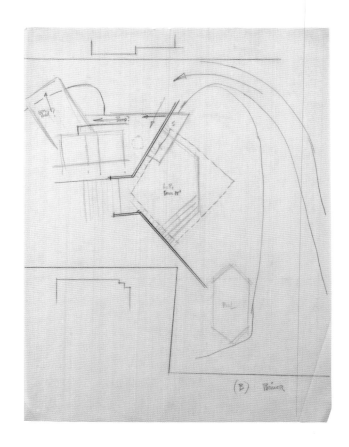

The first ambitious commission in Lautner's career came in 1956, with Kenneth Reiner's Silvertop. Alongside Chemosphere it marks a clear turning point in his work. Reiner, an electrical engineer and inventor, worked in the rapidly expanding wartime aerospace industry, before starting his own company, Kaynar. In 1949 the Reiner family moved into Rudolf Schindler's Guy Wilson House (1939), in the Silver Lake area of Los Angeles, working with Schindler to adapt it. While living there, Reiner purchased an extraordinary piece of land at the top of a nearby hill: views extended east across Silver Lake to the San Gabriel Mountains, and west to the Hollywood Hills and the Griffith Park observatory. Lautner—engaged after a long and exhaustive search—prepared sketches for various schemes to capture the panoramic view. A large, circular glass building, with smaller circular spaces enclosed within, and a glass box angled along the east-west axis were briefly examined. Soon ideas developed of solid walls funneling and framing the eastern and western views, and shielding the private rooms from the central space. With this, the final concept, a space bracketed between two solid walls curving in from and back out to the landscape with a gigantic roof arcing over these, quickly emerged. Originally the roof was to be built in wood, and engineering and framing plans were developed before the idea of a vast concrete shell—first a conventional, later a post-tensioned concrete construction, was proposed. He also designed a cantilevered driveway that caused much resistance from city building inspectors—a horizontal, post-tensioned concrete structure cantilevered off a vertical post-tensioned concrete block wall.

Architect and client both saw the house as a laboratory to develop innovative construction components, which Reiner's company would research and develop. Some of the resulting products were clips to attach the tongue-and-groove wood siding, allowing flexibility as the wood shrank and expanded; hinged baseboards covering electrical outlets;

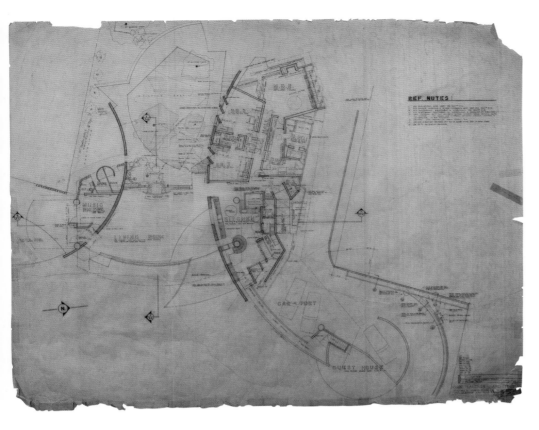

window hardware allowing rotations of 270 degrees; a low-voltage system with sweep controls; optic-eye controls for water faucets; swinging lights, which withdrew into the ceiling when switched off; and a kitchen stove on wheels. Various solutions for the moving glass living room wall were also examined, from lowering the glass into the ground to gathering it, like a sculpture, inside the room.

The long investigation into Silvertop—and especially the discovery of the expressive possibilities of curving concrete—shifted the aesthetics of Lautner's work and dramatically expanded the challenge to his structural imagination and the range of his inquiries into new forms and engineering. Tung-Yen Lin, one of the world's foremost experts on pre-stressed concrete technologies, was brought in as the engineer for the roof structure. In reinforced concrete constructions, the steel absorbs the tension, and the concrete absorbs the compression on the structure. By either pre-stressing the steel before the concrete is poured or post-tensioning it after, with the steel encased in a sleeve that allows it to move within the concrete slab, the structural performance of the steel members is increased greatly, allowing a more economical, and ultimately, more elegant use of the materials. Refining systems patented by the French engineer Eugène Freyssinet, whose methods of anchoring the steel to the concrete had first made pre-stressed methods practical, Lin effectively introduced advanced pre-stressing and post-tensioning to the United States.

During the work on Silvertop, in the spring of 1960, Lautner and Reiner traveled to Europe researching new construction materials and methods. The trip included stops in Portugal, Helsinki (to visit works by Alvar Aalto), Leningrad, Moscow, Vienna, and Italy (where Lautner

*left* Silvertop, Los Angeles, 1963: sketch, plan, preliminary schemes
*above* Silvertop, Los Angeles, 1963: construction drawing, plan, main level
*right* Silvertop, Los Angeles, 1963: construction drawing, plan, roof framing

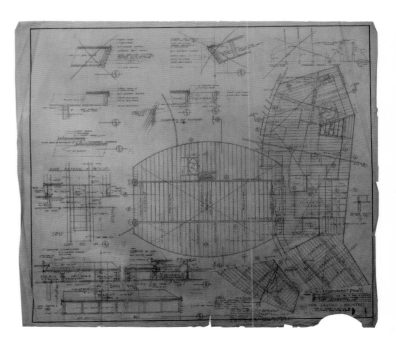

SILVERTOP

Silvertop, Los Angeles, 1963: views during construction of roof

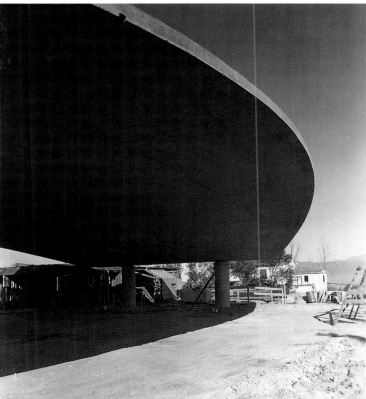

carefully studied Pier Luigi Nervi's Palazzetto dello Sport). Nervi's roof structure for the Palazzetto (1955), a system of load-bearing elements, allowed enormous visual and material lightness. A shell, vast and solid yet delicate, it displays what most intrigued Lautner about Nervi—his expressive formal manifestations of structural logic and his rational yet intuitive approach to engineering. Years later, on a second trip to Italy, Lautner would explore the formal expressionism of Giovanni Michelucci's Chiesa di San Giovanni sull' Autostrada del Sole (1964). On an earlier trip with Reiner, to Mexico, Lautner met Félix Candela and visited several of his projects. Reiner had been introduced to Candela's work through a project for his Kaynar factory, and Lautner would have known of his work as early as May 1957, when a major exhibition was held in Los Angeles. Candela, trained in Madrid, emigrated after the Spanish Civil War to Mexico. His Cosmic Ray Building (1951) in Mexico City, where he reduced the thickness of the concrete shell to a hitherto unimaginable ⅝ inch (15 mm), brought international attention to his work, as did his ongoing research into thin shell and hyperbolic paraboloid concrete structures, in which the concrete formwork of complex curvatures is built entirely from molding it between flat boards, thus achieving fluent forms through relatively simple and inexpensive formwork. Similarly Candela's work on concrete mushrooms, tilting the slabs and bending the symmetrical structures to their limits, opened entirely new worlds of formal explorations in concrete structure.

It is clear that in all these figures, but perhaps in Candela especially, Lautner recognized a kinship, with his own explorations in using concrete shells that date to the start of his postwar career, with the first unbuilt project for the Eisele guesthouse. There, the shell roof emerges as a catenary curve from the ground, while perforations and penetrations in it allow an even and dappled light to filter into the space, converting the massive concrete shell into a delicate filigree (as in Nervi's work).

At the Sheats House, a different geometry for a concrete "cave" is used, and the shell is folded. The structure, tied together with enormous beams below ground, resembles a distorted box. The coffered ceiling is more massive than gravity alone requires: thinner beams would not create the sensation

*left* Giovanni Michelucci, Chiesa di S.Giovanni sull' Autostrada del Sole, Florence, Italy, 1964, photographed by John Lautner
*above left and top right* Pier Luigi Nervi, Palazzetto dello Sport, Rome, 1955, photographed by John Lautner in 1960
*right* Eisele Guesthouse, Los Angeles, California, 1946: construction details: plan, section and details

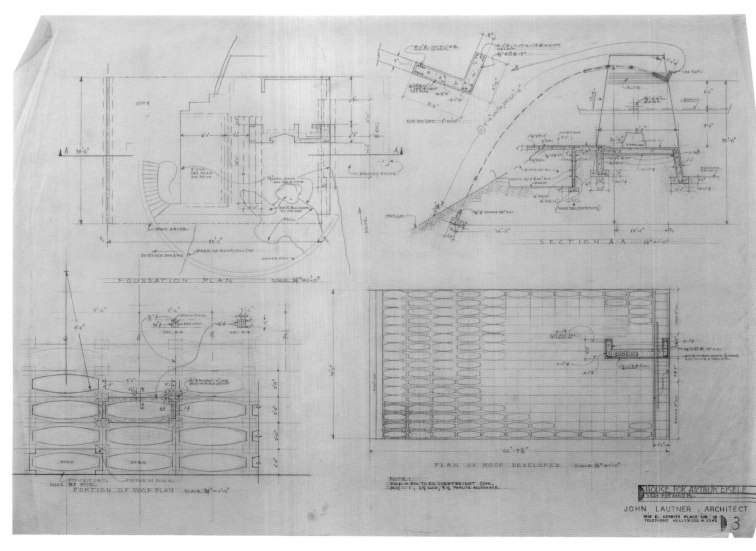

SHEATS HOUSE

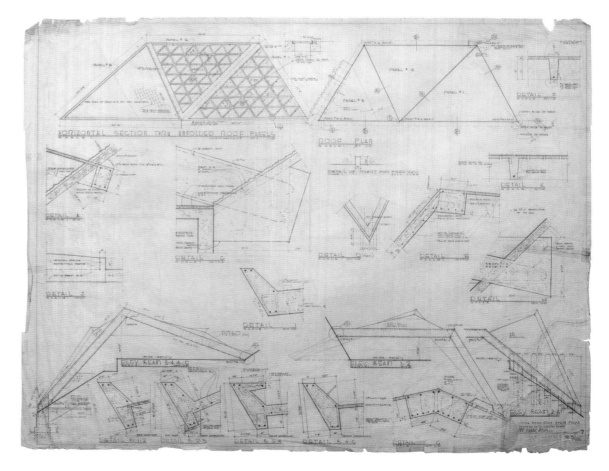

*above* Sheats House, Los Angeles, California, 1963:
views during construction of roof
*right* Sheats House, Los Angeles, California, 1963:
construction drawing, roof structure plan, elevation,
and details
*far right* Sheats House, Los Angeles, California, 1963:
view of swimming pool

Sheats House, Los Angeles, California, 1963: John Lautner
at construction site

*above* Hope House, Palm Springs, California, 1979:
model of preliminary roof structure produced by office
of Félix Candela
*right* Hope House, Palm Springs, California, 1979:
views during construction
*far right* Hope House, Palm Springs, California, 1979

of utter solidity that Lautner sought. Again, though, the mass is lightened by introducing a filtered light. There is a constant tension between conveying and, at times, exaggerating the feeling or sensation of absolute solidity, and then, quite literally, puncturing this solidity with grids of openings and apertures.

The Hope House (1979), originally begun shortly before the Mar Brisas house, was intended to push the formal possibilities of concrete construction even further. The idea of the house as a huge mound—reshaping the topography of its site by adding a form that echoed and reinforced its mountainous surroundings and sheltering within a cavernous space—recurred in Lautner's work.

Originally proposed as a thin shell concrete construction, the Hope House was developed with Candela. But early in the process, at the clients' demand, the same architectural form was awkwardly translated into an enormous steel structure, finished with a cement plaster. It is perhaps this shifting of structural strategy for cost reasons at Hope that prompted Lautner to first propose the roof of Mar Brisas as a steel structure and, once this steel structure proved to be the more costly solution in Mexico, convert this into the massive and completely poured-in-place structure. A similar fate befell the Beyer House, begun in 1973 but halted because of permit complications and revived seven years later at a smaller scale, when earlier and more ambitious plans to build the entire structure in concrete were abandoned in favor of a more economical, and conventional, wooden roof construction.

Aside from Candela, Frei Otto's explorations of asymmetrical systems fascinated Lautner the most. Otto increasingly used his study and observation of natural forms, such as plant structures, to inform his own work, and Lautner studied it with keen interest, visiting the roof structures for the 1972 Munich Olympic stadia. Although most of Lautner's own projects for suspended lightweight or tensile structures remained unbuilt, the Tolstoy House (1961) is an exquisite exception. The roof is a system of cables tautly strung across the land and curved concrete walls, like the bridges of a violin, lift the strings off

HOPE HOUSE

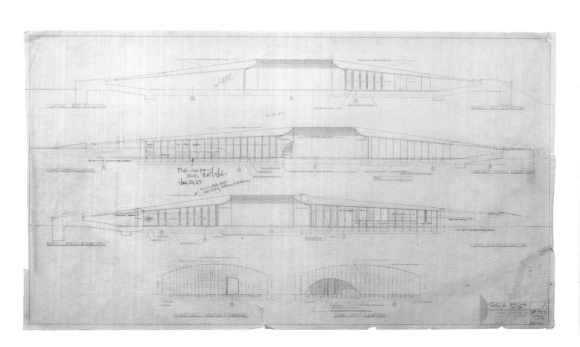

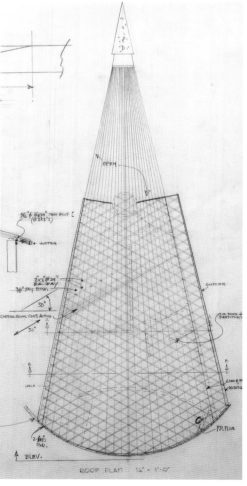

TOLSTOY HOUSE

*above left*  Tolstoy House, Alta Loma, California, 1961: aerial
view and exterior view
*far left*  Tolstoy House, Alta Loma, California, 1961:
construction drawing, elevations
*left*  Tolstoy House, Alta Loma, California, 1961: study, plan
and details of roof structure
*this page*  Tolstoy House, Alta Loma, California, 1961: views
during construction

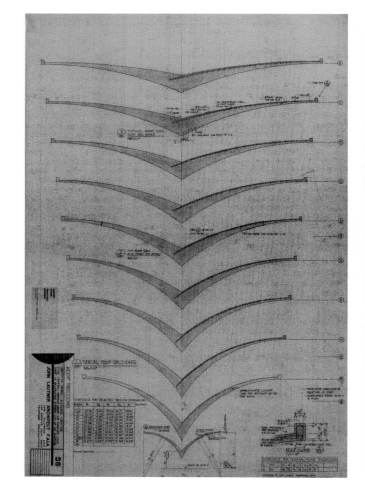

the ground. The tension wire structure is covered with polyurethane foam and a dwelling develops beneath.

After 1972 Lautner consulted principally with the engineer Andrew Nasser, who had worked in the 1950s with Eero Saarinen and came to Lautner's attention as an expert in thin-shell concrete. With this modest, but brilliant, engineer Lautner developed most of the projects in the last twenty years of his career, beginning with an unbuilt nature center (1973) for Griffith Park, in which enormous winglike roofs hover protectively over the three parts of the building. The crease in the roof would give the enormous leaf its structural stability, while the curvature of the roof gently encloses and simultaneously opens up its spaces to the sky.

For the Franklyn project (1973) in Argentina, a series of sculptural supports, like a row of trees, rise from the ground to carry the various levels of the dwelling as well as the immense roofs, which gently curl down to protect the interior space from the harsh sunlight. The living levels and the roof form a gigantic elliptical figure, around which was laid out the client's polo-pony training tracks. Another unbuilt project, the Townsend beach house (1990), again relies on treelike supports to lift the dwelling off its site. This house, however, is a shell, open on one side to the sea, with the floor seamlessly transitioning to concave wall and from the wall to the roof. At the Malibu Cliff House (1990), Lautner's last major project, on which he worked for over a decade, the concrete walls undulate, cant, and slope around the entire property, the private garden essentially becoming the house's main space. A ramp leads up along the outside of one of these walls, crosses through the wall and slips beneath the roof folding out of the perimeter wall. Like the earlier Eisele ski cabin, or the Sheats House, a series of apertures, here in an irregular pattern, bring light through the shell and give the roof a visual lightness. The cavernous shell reads like a delicate membrane and is, in fact, at its apex only four inches thick.

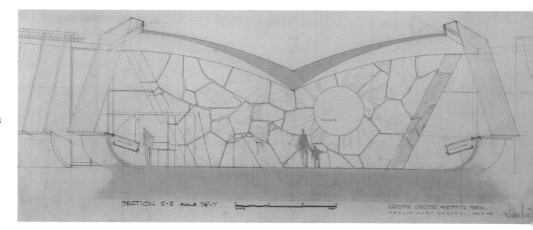

*top* Griffith Park nature center project, Los Angeles, California, 1973: construction drawing, sections of roof structure
*bottom* Griffith Park nature center project, Los Angeles, California, 1973: study, section
*above right* Franklyn house project, Buenos Aires, Argentina, 1973: study model
*right* Franklyn house project, Buenos Aires, Argentina, 1973: construction drawing, sections of structure

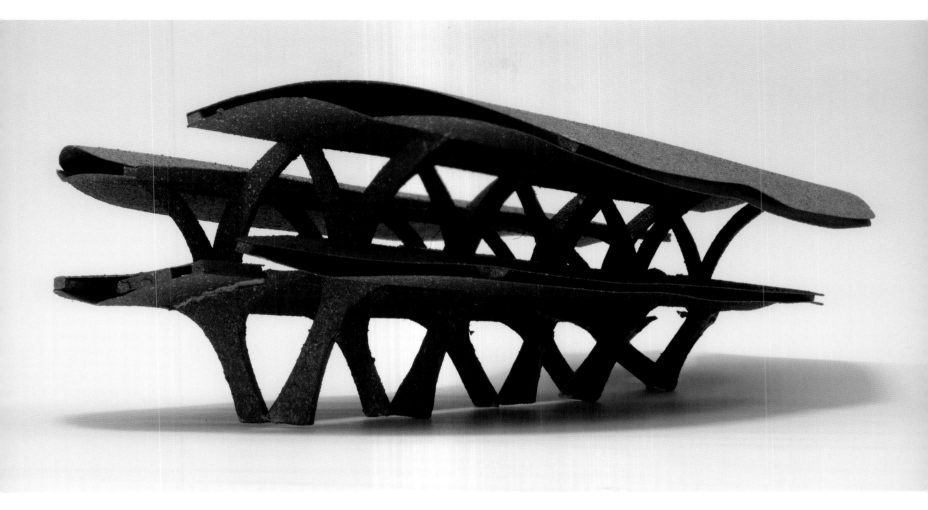

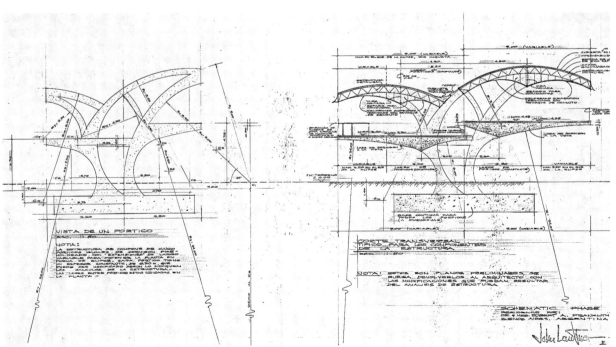

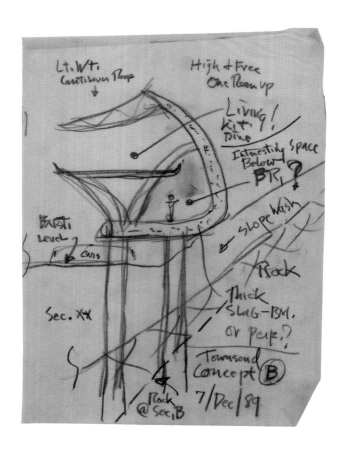

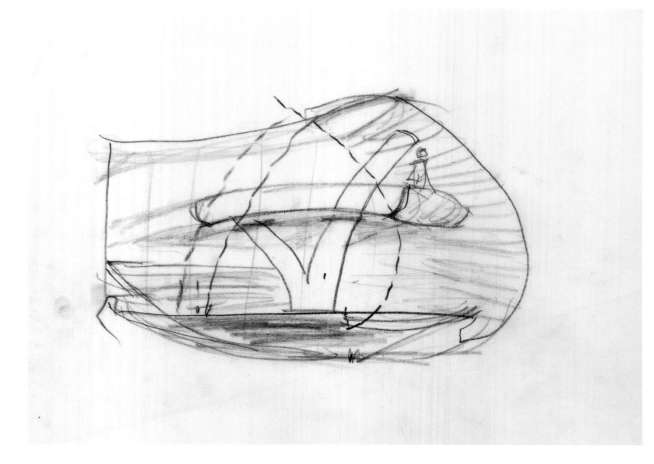

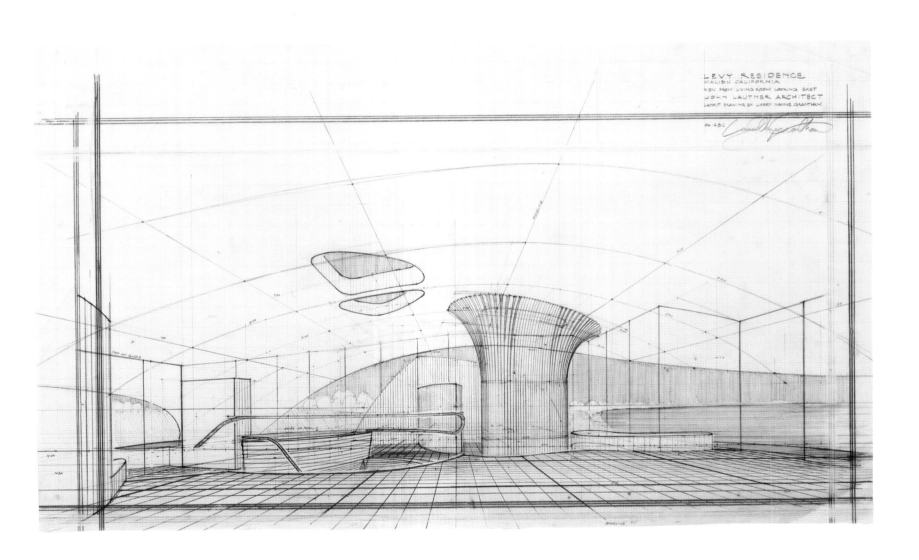

LEVY RESIDENCE
MALIBU CALIFORNIA
VIEW FROM LIVING ROOM LOOKING EAST
JOHN LAUTNER ARCHITECT
LAYOUT DRAWING BY LARRY WAYNE GRANTHAM

*left* Townsend house project, Malibu, California, 1990:
sketch, sections of preliminary scheme
*above* Malibu Cliff House, Malibu, California, 1990: study,
interior perspective

Elrod House, Palm Springs, California, 1968: views of the entry

At the Elrod House (1968) above Palm Springs, a series of walls at the entry act as curved concrete veils to seduce and draw one in from the scorching desert street, through a small enclosed courtyard, and into the cooling embrace of the main space. There, the heavy domed roof ("That heavy stuff," Albert Frey complained) pushes down, while the site's geology is almost violently thrust out of the ground and through the floor.[5] The central space, quiet amid this cataclysm, is captured in between and then slips out to the world around it.

The roof is a shallow cone: a massive concrete tension ring at the base supports nine wide concrete beams that radiate from the center. Between these beams, triangular areas are either covered in heavy concrete (though slightly lifted off to allow a sliver of light), or completely glazed (originally with crystalline, frameless glass), open to the view of the mountains above and the sky beyond. The result of this handling of light, the precise openings, and the concealed steel supports, is that the mass of the roof miraculously appears to float, or hover, weightlessly. From the main body of the house, at the edge of the desert plateau, a linear master bedroom suite stretches to one side along the cliff and into the rocks, and to the other side a terrace extends. This is a place from which to contemplate the world and its desert light, softly caressing the land at dawn, blinding at midday, and turning to complete darkness by night, intensified by the black expanse of the slate floor inside.

ELROD HOUSE

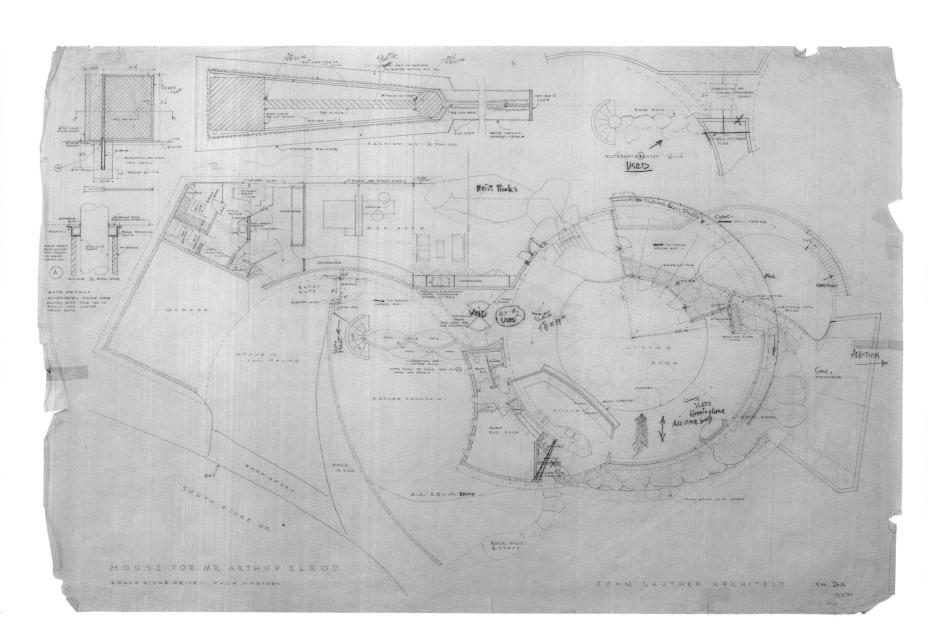

HOUSE FOR MR. ARTHUR ELROD

SOUTH RIDGE DRIVE · PALM SPRINGS

JOHN LAUTNER ARCHITECT      SH. 2A

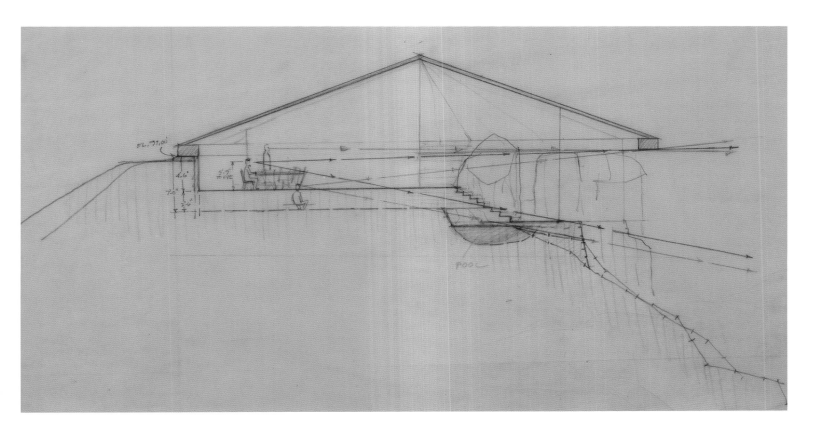

previous spread  Elrod House, Palm Springs, California, 1968:
interior view of main space
left  Elrod House, Palm Springs, California, 1968: construction
drawing, plan and details of main level and gate
above  Elrod House, Palm Springs, California, 1968: study, section
right  Elrod House, Palm Springs, California, 1968: study model

Elrod House, Palm Springs, California, 1968

The building, barely a piece of architecture, is but a form—a mound—in the landscape, created by a fragment of an immense concrete sphere being pressed into—or out of—the earth. Between the crust of the earth and this sheltering firmament, not one wall touching the ceiling, is created the world of the Turner House (1982), a space where one is both sheltered from and exposed to the landscape.

Like Mar Brisas, the space is captured by an immense concrete roof, concave rather than convex, and a new ground, more geometrically complex and with private cavern-like areas carved out of it. The main space, reached, as in the Walstrom House, through a carefully choreographed spatial sequence that leads from the lower floor entrance up a narrow, curved stair to the borrowed landscape, removed and precisely framed. And like the Pearlman Mountain Cabin, the house relates to a basic human shelter—here, not the primitive hut, but a cave. Key concepts of Lautner's work are illustrated in the Turner House: pushing the limits of form and structure; the idea of building as an extension into and from the landscape; and a formal fluidity and plasticity that was ahead of its time—ahead, in fact, of reasonable techniques to achieve it. In the last years of his career, Lautner imagined and explored new worlds of forms—worlds that the architectural discourse only now, a quarter century later, inhabits.

Turner House, Aspen, Colorado, 1982: views
during construction

TURNER HOUSE

Turner House, Aspen, Colorado, 1982:
exterior during construction

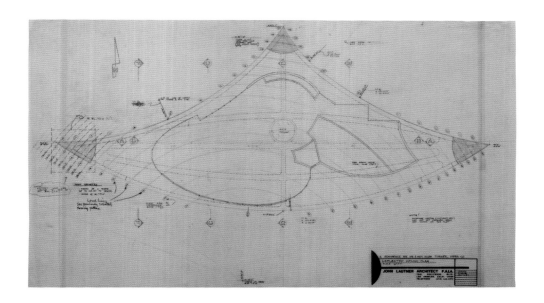

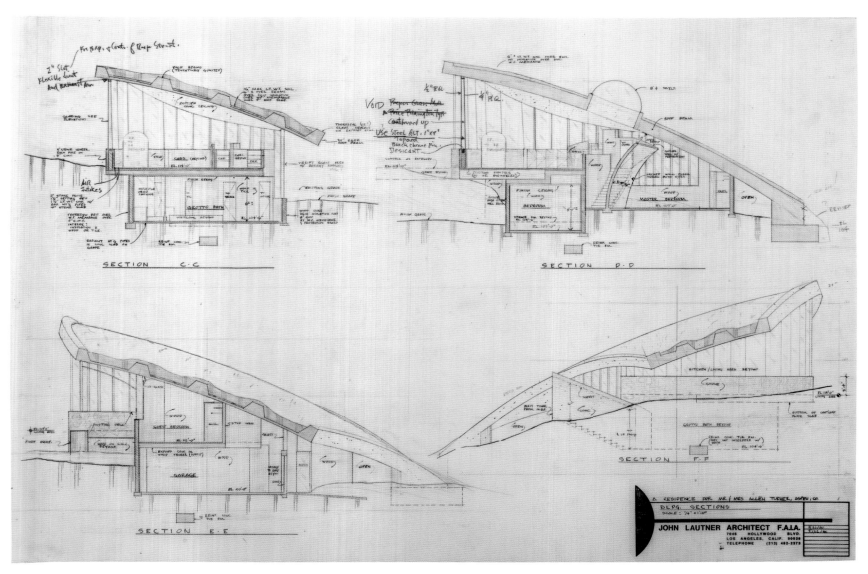

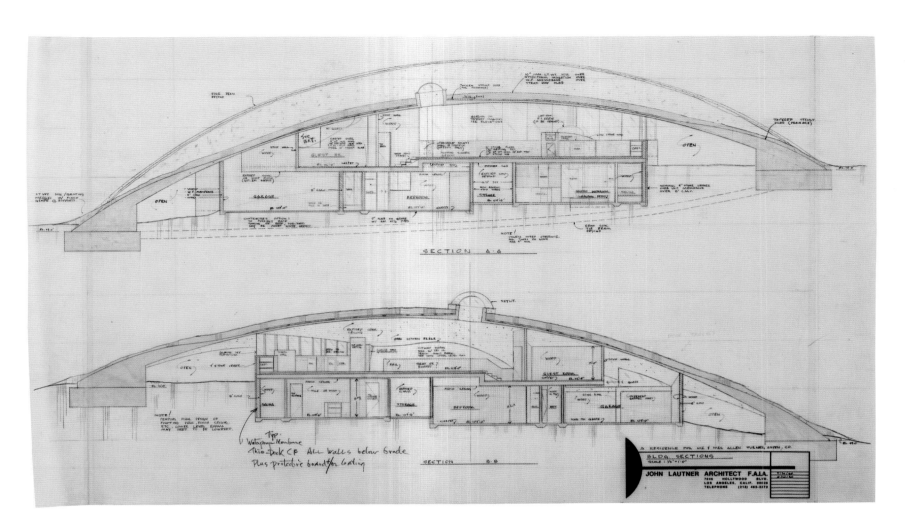

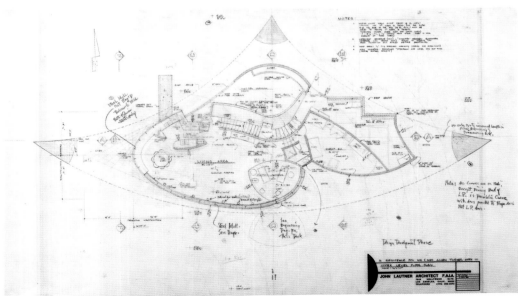

*top left* Turner House, Aspen, Colorado, 1982: construction drawing, roof plan

*bottom left* Turner House, Aspen, Colorado, 1982: construction drawing, sections and elevations

*above* Turner House, Aspen, Colorado, 1982: construction drawing, sections

*right* Turner House, Aspen, Colorado, 1982: construction drawing, main level plan

Turner House, Aspen, Colorado, 1982

1 The exact wording and spelling in Lautner's meeting notes is "[Below] . . . 3 servants . . .
5 Kids . . . 1 Master . . . Large open Room" and "Min. Grading," "Disappearing Clg."

2 The Wolff Cabin project was actually built, but without John Lautner's involvement.

3 Malibu Cliff House is sometimes referred to as the Levy House.

4 *Robert Maillart: Engineer* (exhibition), New York, Museum of Modern Art, 24 June–13
October, 1947.

5 Jennifer Golub, *Albert Frey: Houses 1 + 2* (Princeton Architectural Press: New York, 1998):
78. The full passage, from an interview Golub conducted with Frey, is:

"Golub: Your material choices are all very light, thin almost delicate, though sturdy and
structural. When I think of your regional contemporaries—John Lautner's heavy concrete or
Craig Ellwood's steel beams—it seems as if you have proven how so much construction is
unnecessary. Is that an expression of economy or an aesthetic preference?

"Frey: A sense of economy and taking advantage of the latest inventions. That's an
invention, this corrugated metal and so on. I think it doesn't make sense to have heavy concrete overhead. Why lift all that heavy stuff up there? I'm sure it's more expensive too—particularly concrete: you have to form it. I always liked the lightness of things. The sheet-metal
people put up the roof: it took them a day. And then I put these panels up on the insulation
myself. If you have concrete, they actually have to build a whole structure to support it. It
doesn't make sense. Concrete is fine in relation to the ground. It's an earth material."

This essay drew on Lautner's project documents and files, and structural engineer-
ing files in the John Lautner Archive, The John Lautner Foundation (by the time book is
published, these materials will be at the Getty); David P. Billigton, *Robert Maillart's Bridges:
The Art of Engineering* (Princeton University Press: New York, 1979); Paolo Desideri, "Pier
Luigi Nervi," *Verlag für Architectur* (Artemis: Zürich, 1982); Barbara Lamprecht, "The Great
American Stud," *Metropolis* (October 1998); and August Sarnitz, *R. M. Schindler, Architekt*
(Edition Christian Brandstätter: Vienna, 1986).

During 1994 and 1995, the author corresponded with Octavia Walstrom, Judith
Lautner, Julia Strickland, Louis Wiehle, Leonard Malin, Guy Zebert, Helena Arahuete, Ken
Reiner, and Andrew Nasser. Excerpts from these conversations were published in Frank
Escher, ed., "A Tribute to John Lautner," *Journal of the Taliesin Fellows*, Issue 18, Summer
1995.

From 1992 to 1994, the author had conversations with John Lautner, Karol Lautner
Peterson, Julia Strickland, Douglas and Octavia Walstrom, Leonard Malin, John de la Vaux,
Benedikt Taschen, Andrew Nasser, Vaughan Trammell, Judith Lautner (interview on 21
April 2007), Helena Arahuete (interview on 12 April 2007), Guy Zebert (interview on 27
October 2000), Ken Reiner (interview 27 October 2000), Nancy Pearlman (interview on 10
March 2007), John Contini (interview on 6 March 2007), and Nora Contini (interview on 6
March 2007).

# SELECTED BIOGRAPHY 1911–94

| | |
|---|---|
| 1911 | Born July 16, Marquette, Michigan, to "Vida" Cathleen Gallagher, an artist and schoolteacher, and John Edward Lautner, founding head of German, French, and social studies at Northern State Normal School (renamed Northern State Teachers College, then Northern Michigan University) |
| 1923–28 | Design and construction of log cabin "Midgaard" as "a family project"—Lautner's first experience of building |
| 1933 | Graduates with a liberal arts degree from Northern State Teachers College |
| 1933 | Joins Frank Lloyd Wright's Taliesin Fellowship with fiancée Mary ("Marybud") F. Roberts |
| 1934 | Marries Mary F. Roberts of Marquette, Michigan, daughter of Abby Beecher Roberts, the owner of Deertrack summer resort in Marquette, Michigan |
| 1935 | First winter season with Taliesin Fellowship in Scottsdale, Arizona; exhibits Wright's Broadacre City project in Marquette, Michigan. |
| 1936–38 | Supervises construction of Wright's house for Abby Beecher Roberts at Deertrack in Marquette, Michigan, and Herbert Johnson (Wingspread) in Wind Point, Wisconsin |
| 1938 | Leaves Taliesin Fellowship and moves to Los Angeles, working both in independent design practice and in association with Wright; daughter Karol Lautner born |
| 1940 | First national publication of works as independent designer, notably "A Hillside Redwood House Designed by John Lautner," *California Arts and Architecture* 57 (June–July) |
| 1942 | Son Michael John Lautner born |
| 1943 | Joins Structon Company to work on wartime military construction and engineering projects in California; professional association with Wright ends |
| 1944 | Daughter Mary Beecher Lautner born |
| 1944 | Pursues joint ventures with architects Samuel Reisbord and Whitney R. Smith, Pasadena, California; joins architectural firm of Douglas Honnold, Los Angeles, California, as design associate |
| 1946 | Daughter Judith Lautner born |
| 1947 | Ends collaboration with Honnold; Lautner establishes his own design practice at El Cerrito Place, Los Angeles, California; separates and divorces from Marybud |
| 1948 | Marries Elizabeth Gilman Honnold; first compendium of work published in *Arts and Architecture*: "Roof Structures by John Lautner, Designer" and "Drive-In Restaurant, John Lautner, Designer," *Arts and Architecture* 65 (June) |
| 1950 | Included in exhibition of sixteen Southern California architects at Scripps College, Claremont, California |
| 1952 | Lautner obtains his architecture license |
| 1960 | Studio and home destroyed by fire; re-establishes office on Hollywood Boulevard, Los Angeles, California |
| 1963 | Exhibition *Architect: John Lautner* at Mount San Antonio College, Walnut, California, and at Art Center College of Los Angeles, Pasadena, California |
| 1965 | Compendium of work with commentary by Esther McCoy, "West Coast Architects V. John Lautner," *Arts and Architecture* 82 (August) |
| 1966 | Exhibition at the University of Kentucky, Lexington, Kentucky |
| 1967 | Exhibition at the California State College, Los Angeles, California |
| 1971 | Named Fellow of American Institute of Architects; interview by Arthur Mann, "The Architect's Perspective," *Architectural Digest* 28 (July/August) |
| 1973 | Exhibition *A View of California Architecture, 1960–1976* at San Francisco Museum of Modern Art; exhibition catalogue published |
| 1974 | Exhibition *Three Worlds of Los Angeles* and catalogue organized by Beata Inaya, sponsored by the United States Information Agency and Cultural Centers in Europe; exhibition traveled widely in Europe |
| 1976 | Exhibition *Los Angeles 12* at Pacific Design Center, Los Angeles, and California State Polytechnic, Pomona, California; exhibition catalogue published |
| 1979 | Elizabeth Honnold dies |
| 1981 | Survey of work in Pierluigi Bonvicini, *John Lautner: Architettura Organico–Sperimentale* (Bari, Italy: Edizioni Dedalo Spa) |
| 1982 | Marries Francisca Hernandez |
| 1985 | Exhibition *John Lautner* at Schindler House, Los Angeles; interview in *Opus Incertum*, vol. 1 (April), Journal of the University of Texas at Austin |
| 1986 | Compendium of work with commentary by Alan Hess "The Redoubtable Mr. Lautner," *L.A. Style* 11 (October) |
| 1987 | Compendium of work published with commentary by Renato Pedio in "Sette Opere di John Lautner in California, Colorado, e Messico," *L'Architettura XXXIII* (January), and Dominique Lyon, "John Lautner: An American Dream," *L'Architecture d'Aujourd'hui* 250 (April) |
| 1989 | Published in Diana Rico, "Master of Form: Architect John Lautner, L.A.'s Enduring Maverick," *Los Angeles* (November) |
| 1990 | Published in Henry Whiting, "Living History: The Architecture of John Lautner," *Designers West* 37 (February) |
| 1991 | Exhibition *John Lautner* at Hochschule für Angewandte Kunst, Vienna, Austria; Harvard Graduate School of Design, Harvard University, Cambridge, Massachusetts; Graham Foundation for Advanced Studies in the Fine Arts, Chicago, Illinois; feature-length documentary film with commentary and interview directed by Bette Jean Cohen, *The Spirit in Architecture, John Lautner*; Henry Whiting, "50 Years in Los Angeles: John Lautner's Transcendental Architecture." *Global Architecture* [Tokyo] 32 (July); Barbara-Ann Campbell "Solid and Free," interview in *The Architectural Review*, v.189 (August) |
| 1992 | Exhibition *John Lautner* travels to Emily Carr College of Art and Design, Vancouver, British Columbia, and the National Institute of Architectural Education, New York, New York |
| 1993 | Awarded Gold Medal of the American Institute of Architects, Los Angeles Chapter, on November 17 |
| 1994 | *John Lautner, Architect*, first and final monograph published (London and Zurich: Artemis), edited by Frank Escher; October 24, John Lautner dies, Los Angeles, California |

# SELECTED PROJECTS

MIDGAARD 1923–28, Middle Island Point, MI
Family cabin built with parents, sister, and students

STURGES HOUSE 1939, Los Angeles, CA
Frank Lloyd Wright with John Lautner

RALPH JESTER HOUSE PROJECT* 1938–39, Scottsdale, AZ
Frank Lloyd Wright with John Lautner

GREEN HOUSE PROJECT* 1940–41, Los Angeles, CA
Frank Lloyd Wright with John Lautner

LAUTNER HOUSE 1940, Los Angeles, CA

EAGLEFEATHER (ARCH OBOLER ESTATE) 1940–41, Los Angeles, CA
Frank Lloyd Wright with John Lautner and Lloyd Wright

BELL HOUSE 1940, Los Angeles, CA

SPRINGER HOUSE 1940, Los Angeles, CA

EISELE GUESTHOUSE,1946, Los Angeles, CA

MAUER HOUSE 1946, Los Angeles, CA

CARLING HOUSE 1947 (remodeled 1991), Los Angeles, CA

DESERT HOT SPRINGS MOTEL (BUBBLING WELLS RESORT)
1947, Desert Hot Springs, CA

GANTVOORT HOUSE 1947, Flintridge, CA

HENRY'S RESTAURANT 1947, Glendale, CA

JACOBSEN HOUSE 1947, Los Angeles, CA

POLIN HOUSE 1947, Los Angeles, CA

"L'HORIZON" APARTMENTS (SHEATS) 1948, Los Angeles, CA

ABBOT APARTMENTS PROJECT* 1948, Los Angeles, CA

FERBER HOUSE PROJECT* 1948, Altadena, CA

STIFF HOUSE PROJECT* 1948, Los Angeles, CA

ROSS HOUSE PROJECT* 1948, Los Angeles, CA

SALKIN HOUSE PROJECT* 1948, Los Angeles, CA

LINCOLN ZEPHYR SHOWROOM 1948, Glendale, CA

VALLEY ESCROW COMPANY OFFICES 1948, Sherman Oaks, CA

GOOGIE'S COFFEE HOUSE 1949, Los Angeles, CA

UPA STUDIOS 1949, Burbank, CA

SCHAFFER HOUSE 1949, Montrose, CA

DAHLSTROM HOUSE 1949, Pasadena, CA

FOSTER HOUSE 1950, Sherman Oaks, CA

HARVEY HOUSE 1950, Los Angeles, CA

SHUSETT HOUSE 1950, Los Angeles, CA

CAPLIS DRIVE-IN RESTAURANT PROJECT* 1952, Hawthorne, CA

BERGREN HOUSE 1953, Los Angeles, CA

TYLER HOUSE 1953, Los Angeles, CA

BEACHWOOD MARKET 1954, Los Angeles, CA

CONECO CORPORATION HOUSE 1954, Los Angeles, CA

HARPEL HOUSE 1956, Los Angeles, CA

SPEER CONTRACTORS OFFICE BUILDING 1956, Los Angeles, CA

HENRY'S RESTAURANT 1957, Pomona, CA

PEARLMAN MOUNTAIN CABIN 1957, Idyllwild, CA

HATHERALL HOUSE 1958, Sun Valley, CA

PEARLMAN HOUSE PROJECT* 1958, Santa Ana, CA

HENRY'S RESTAURANT 1959, Alhambra, CA

CONCANNON HOUSE 1960 (demolished 2002), Los Angeles, CA

CHEMOSPHERE (MALIN) 1960, Los Angeles, CA

MIDTOWN SCHOOL 1960, Los Angeles, CA

TOLSTOY HOUSE 1961, Alta Loma, CA

WOLFF HOUSE 1961 (addition 1963), Los Angeles, CA

GARCIA HOUSE 1962, Los Angeles, CA

SHEATS HOUSE (NOW SHEATS/GOLDSTEIN) 1963, Los Angeles, CA

SILVERTOP (REINER) 1963, Los Angeles, CA

ALTO CAPISTRANO PROJECT* 1963–1969, San Juan Capistrano, CA

GOLDSMITH HOUSE 1964, Los Angeles, CA

JOHNSON HOUSE 1965, Laguna Beach, CA

MISBIN HOUSE PROJECT* 1968, Los Angeles, CA

HARPEL HOUSE 1966, Anchorage, AK

ELROD HOUSE 1968, Palm Springs, CA

STEVENS HOUSE 1968, Malibu, CA

ZIMMERMAN HOUSE 1968 (addition 1982), Los Angeles, CA

LABORATORY AND LIVING QUARTERS FOR OWENS VALLEY
OBSERVATORY (CAL TECH PROJECT)* 1968, Pasadena, CA

PETERS HOUSE PROJECT* 1968, Thousand Oaks, CA

WALSTROM HOUSE 1969, Los Angeles, CA

FAMILIAN HOUSE 1971, Los Angeles, CA

MAR BRISAS 1973, Acapulco, Mexico

FRANKLYN HOUSE PROJECT* 1973, Buenos Aires, Argentina

GRIFFITH PARK NATURE CENTER PROJECT* 1973, Los Angeles, CA

LAUTNER MOUNTAIN CABIN PROJECT* 1974, Three Rivers, CA

WOLFF MOUNTAIN CABIN PROJECT 1975, Idyllwild, CA

FAMILIAN BEACH HOUSE PROJECT* 1976, Malibu, CA

SEGEL HOUSE 1979, Malibu, CA

HOPE HOUSE 1979, Palm Springs, CA

TURNER CONDOMINIUMS PROJECT* 1981, Marina Del Rey, CA

TURNER HOUSE 1982, Aspen, CO

SCHWIMMER HOUSE 1982, Los Angeles, CA

KRAUSE HOUSE 1982, Malibu, CA

BEYER HOUSE 1983, Malibu, CA

ROVEN HOUSE PROJECT* 1986, Los Angeles, CA

HAAGEN BEACH CABIN PROJECT* 1988, Malibu, CA

GOLDSTEIN OFFICES 1989, Los Angeles, CA

MALIBU CLIFF HOUSE 1990, Malibu, CA

MILES DAVIS SWIMMING POOL PROJECT* 1990, Malibu, CA

TOWNSEND HOUSE PROJECT* 1990, Malibu, CA

MARINA FINE ARTS 1991, Marina Del Rey, CA

*NOT BUILT

# ILLUSTRATION CREDITS

# INDEX

*Note: Page numbers in italic indicate photographs and drawings.*

# NOTES ON THE AUTHORS

Nicholas Olsberg is a cultural historian with a particular interest in the visible documents of modern societies—written, drawn, photographed, filmed, collected, or built—and of the pattern of manners and ideas captured within them. He was formerly director of the Canadian Centre for Architecture in Montreal (CCA). Olsberg holds an honors degree in modern history from Oxford University and a doctorate in American history from the University of South Carolina. Olsberg has also worked as an archivist for the Getty Center, the University of Massachusetts Boston, the Commonwealth of Massachusetts, Johns Hopkins University, and the Colonial and State Records of South Carolina.

Jean-Louis Cohen is Sheldon H. Solow Professor in the History of Architecture at New York University's Institute of Fine Arts, where he has taught since 1993. Cohen's research activity has focused on twentieth-century architecture and urban planning, in particular German and Soviet architectural cultures, colonial situations in North Africa, Le Corbusier's work, and the planning history of Paris. After studying architecture and history in Paris, Cohen directed the Architectural Research Program at the French Ministry of Housing, and held a research professorship from 1983 to 1996 at the School of Architecture Paris-Villemin. In 1997, the French Minister of Culture invited Cohen to create the Cité de l'architecture, a museum, research, and exhibition center in the Palais de Chaillot in Paris. He has curated numerous exhibitions and authored many books, including *Le Corbusier and the Mystique of the USSR* (1992), *Scenes of the World to Come* (1995), and *Casablanca: Colonial Myths and Architectural Ventures* (2002).

Frank Escher, trained at the ETH (Swiss Federal Institute of Technology) in Zurich, Switzerland, practices architecture in Los Angeles. He is a principal in the firm Escher GuneWardena. From 1991 to 1994, he worked with John Lautner to produce the architect's first monograph, *John Lautner, Architect*. Escher is the administrator for the John Lautner Archives, serves on the board of directors of the John Lautner Foundation and has lectured extensively on Lautner's work in the United States and abroad. He has served as president, and is currently on the advisory board of the Los Angeles Forum for Architecture and Urban Design. Escher has lectured in various forums, including the Cooper Hewitt National Design Conference, the 2006 Architectural League's "Emerging Voices" series, and at California Polytechnic University in Pomona, where he is a visiting faculty member.